More Praise for *Locked Down, Locked Out*

"*Locked Down, Locked Out* paints a searing por▨▨▨▨ of mass incarceration, both on prisoners and o▨ ▨▨▨▨ ▨▨▨▨▨▨▨, ▨▨▨ ▨▨▨▨▨▨ compellingly—provides hope that collectively we can create a more humane world freed of prisons. Read this deeply personal and political call to end the shameful inhumanity of our prison nation."

—Dorothy Roberts, author of *Shattered Bonds* and *Killing the Black Body*

"This moving book makes a very important intervention into both the popular understanding and the political discussions about mass imprisonment. In her riveting descriptions of what happens to families caught in the long reach of the prison nation, Schenwar makes a compelling case for prison abolition and reinvestment in communities. This book will change both what we understand about injustice and how we work for more logical and effective solutions."

—Beth E. Richie, author of *Arrested Justice*

"The prime excuse for imprisoning people—to punish wrongdoers and serve as a deterrent to others—is simply incorrect and unworkable...Maya Schenwar makes a powerful argument that our resources can better be utilized to provide treatment, education, restorative justice practices, healing circles, the arts, and more. I salute Maya and her courage. This book should stand out as key to finally ending the imprisoning of America."

—Luis J. Rodriguez, author of *Always Running* and *Hearts and Hands*

"*Locked Down, Locked Out* may be the best and most deeply moving book yet published on mass incarceration in the United States. Everyone who wants to understand what it means for the United States to recover a sense of dignity, justice, and the need for collective action should read this book."

—Henry A. Giroux, author of *Disposable Youth* and *Twilight of the Social*

"I read *Locked Down, Locked Out* ravenously, surprised and enlightened on every page. It is a searing portrayal of waywardness and redemption, justice arrested and deliverance detained. No one has narrated and illuminated the collateral damage of our carceral state more powerfully than Maya Schenwar."

—Bill Ayers, author of *Fugitive Days* and *Public Enemy*

"If *Locked Down, Locked Out* had been just about Maya's family's experience with her sister's struggles with incarceration, it would have been worth the read. But Maya has given us more: the narratives of others and how incarceration weaves itself around the lives of those inside and out until all are entangled in the vicious web. She gives those whose names we have forgotten their names back and gives us all reason to destroy what has been this nation's consistent and embarrassing failure."

—R. Dwayne Betts, author of *A Question of Freedom*

"Schenwar doesn't simply elucidate the many ways in which prisons destroy families and communities; she also brings readers into the everyday workings of real-life projects that begin to answer this question. Anyone who has ever felt concerned about the safety of our communities should read this book."
—**Victoria Law, author of *Resistance behind Bars***

"Maya Schenwar's authentic and compelling writing gives a glimpse into the lives of people who are trapped in the criminal justice system. Among books that aim to narrow the gap between law and justice, this is one of the finest."
—**Kathy Kelly, Nobel Peace Prize nominee and author of *Other Lands Have Dreams***

"*Locked Down, Locked Out* is a much-needed look at systems of social control with a big-picture perspective. A must-read."
—**Joseph "Jazz" Hayden, founder of the Campaign to End the New Jim Crow**

"Maya Schenwar's book is a welcome contribution to the growing body of literature on mass incarceration. Read it and learn not only about how the criminal (in)justice system works and whom it affects but also where you fit into it. With lucidity and courage, Schenwar treats her subject in its entirety, helping us see the role played by those outside the walls."
—**Laura Whitehorn, former political prisoner and editor of *The War Before***

"Maya Schenwar proves prisons are not the solutions society should seek but rather that we should see them as the problem—and take steps to restructure society to bring healing to communities and families."
—**Dolores Canales, founder of California Families Against Solitary Confinement**

"*Locked Down, Locked Out* does a remarkable thing: it provides a human audit of an inhuman system. Schenwar takes us on a harrowing, inspiring journey through the horrors of the prison nation, the effects that reverberate far beyond the prison walls, and the creative brilliance animating contemporary movements for justice."
—**Dan Berger, author of *Captive Nation* and *The Struggle Within***

"Maya Schenwar's story brings compassion into the picture, helping us understand our colossal failure in using prisons to warehouse people most in need of healing."
—**Andrea James, author of *Upper Bunkies Unite* and founder of Families for Justice as Healing**

"With vivid candor, *Locked Down, Locked Out* gets to the heart of one of the greatest tragedies of the prison system: the breakup of families. An enlightening journey."
—**Deborah Jiang-Stein, author of *Prison Baby***

Locked Down,
Locked Out

Locked Down, Locked Out

Why Prison Doesn't Work— and How We Can Do Better

MAYA SCHENWAR

Berrett–Koehler Publishers, Inc.
San Francisco
a BK Currents book

Berrett-Koehler Publishers, Inc.
1333 Broadway, Suite 1000
Oakland, CA 94612-1921
Tel: (510) 817-2277   Fax: (510) 817-2278
www.bkconnection.com

Ordering Information

Quantity sales. Special discounts are available on quantity purchases by corporations, associations, and
others. For details, contact the "Special Sales Department" at the Berrett-Koehler address above.
Individual sales. Berrett-Koehler publications are available through most bookstores. They can also be ordered directly from Berrett-Koehler: Tel: (800) 929-2929; Fax: (802) 864-7626; www.bkconnection.com.
Orders for college textbook/course adoption use. Please contact Berrett-Koehler: Tel: (800) 929-2929;
Fax: (802) 864-7626.
Orders by U.S. trade bookstores and wholesalers. Please contact Ingram Publisher Services, Tel: (800)
509-4887; Fax: (800) 838-1149; E-mail: customer.service@ingrampublisherservices.com; or visit www.
ingrampublisherservices.com/Ordering for details about electronic ordering.

Berrett-Koehler and the BK logo are registered trademarks of
Berrett-Koehler Publishers, Inc.

Printed in the United States of America

Berrett-Koehler books are printed on long-lasting acid-free paper. When it is available, we choose paper that has been manufactured by environmentally responsible processes. These may include using trees
grown in sustainable forests, incorporating recycled paper, minimizing chlorine in bleaching, or recycling
the energy produced at the paper mill.

Library of Congress Cataloging-in-Publication Data
Schenwar, Maya.
Locked down, locked out : why prison doesn't work and how we can do better / Maya Schenwar.
    pages cm
ISBN 978-1-62656-269-1 (paperback)
1. Imprisonment--United States. 2. Alternatives to imprisonment--United States. 3. Corrections--United
States. 4. Criminals--Rehabilitation--United States. 5. Justice, Administration of--United States. I. Title.
    HV9471.S34 2014
    364.60973--dc23
                    2014021463
First Edition
18 17 16 15   10 9 8 7 6 5 4 3 2

Project management, design, and composition by Steven Hiatt / Hiatt & Dragon, San Francisco
Copyediting: Steven Hiatt   Proofreading: Tom Hassett   Cover Design: Irene Morris Design—
Cover photo: Ben Kraus

For my sister

A truly free society must not include a "peace" which oppresses us. We must learn on our own terms what peace and freedom mean together.

—*Petra Karin Kelly*

Contents

Introduction

Into the Hole

"Shit, shit, shit, shit, *shit*!" I'm crying with my mother over the phone. It's late evening, December 25, 2012, and Kayla,* my only sister and best friend, has been arrested for the seventh time in the past six years. She's in jail again—and this time, we're sort of hoping she'll stay there. "If she asks," I tell Mom, "I'm not bailing her out."

"Well, you know *we're* not," Mom says, her voice low and far away, a weary echo of words uttered in months and years past. "If she's in there, at least she'll be safe."

Jail, we agree, may be the only place that can save Kayla's life, staving off her burning dependency on heroin. Neither of us acknowledges that regardless of whether Kayla stays clean while incarcerated, sooner or later she'll be getting out.

"Do we know what she's in for?" I ask Mom.

---

* The names of several people have been changed in this book to protect privacy where necessary. These names are marked with an asterisk on first mention.

"Does it matter?"

I think of Kayla, cuffed and listless, being dragged through the doors of the Cook County Jail, catching the eyes of women she's known before—in court, on the street, in juvenile detention, in jail, in prison. I wonder whether a part of her is relieved to be back.

Later, when I pick up the phone and hear a robotic voice announce, "You have a collect call from the Cook County Jail: press five to take the call," I press the hang-up button and get into bed.

The Hole

My attitude toward Kayla's incarceration was born out of desperation. She had overdosed three times within two months, passing out on the street, awakening in abandoned buildings or crowded hospitals, her pulse barely ticking. Yet my wish chafed against not only my love for her, but also my politics, my ideals, my sense of justice and truth. After all, I run a social justice–based news organization and have denounced the colossus that is the prison-industrial complex for as long as I can remember. For nearly a decade, I've corresponded with a number of people in prison, as both interviewees and pen pals, and I've learned much from them about the violence and hopelessness of the system. My understandings of the power structures that create prisons have been guided by the work of people like activist and scholar Angela Davis, a staunch prison abolitionist. How could I reconcile my wholehearted opposition to the prison-industrial complex with a desire to see my own sister locked up?

When I look back on that time, I can only comprehend it by acknowledging the insidious, persistent role that prison occupied in my mind. It was closely connected to the role it occupies in larger society: Incarceration serves as the default answer to many of the worst social problems plaguing this country—not because it solves them, but because it buries them. By isolating and disappearing millions of Americans (more than 2.3 million, making us the most incarcerated nation on the planet), prison conveniently disappears deeply rooted issues that society—or rather, those with power in society—would rather not attend to.

"Prison," writes Angela Davis, "performs a feat of magic." As massive numbers of homeless, hungry, unemployed, drug-addicted, illiterate, and mentally ill people vanish behind its walls, the social problems of extreme poverty, homelessness, hunger, unemployment, drug addiction, illiteracy, and mental illness become more ignorable, too. But, as Davis notes, "prisons do not disappear problems, they disappear human beings."[1] And the caging and erasure of those human beings, mostly people of color and poor people, perpetuates a cycle in which large groups are cut off from "mainstream society" and denied the freedoms, opportunities, civic dignity, and basic needs that allow them a good life.

In many jails and prisons, incarcerated people are tossed into a dank, dungeon-like solitary confinement cell when they are determined to have "misbehaved." It's dubbed "the Hole." Isolated and dark, it shuts out almost all communication with fellow prisoners and the outside. Guards control the terms of confinement and the channels—if any—by which words can travel in and out. The Hole presents a stark symbol of the institution of prison in its entirety, which functions on the tenets of disappearance, isolation, and disposability. The "solution" to our social problems—the mechanism that's supposed to "keep things together"—amounts to destruction: the disposal of vast numbers of human beings, the breaking down of families, and the shattering of communities. Prison is tearing society apart.

This country's most marginalized communities bear the overwhelming brunt of the devastation. But ultimately we are all caught up in the destruction, as the politics of isolation ruptures the human bonds that could otherwise hold together a safer, healthier, more just society.

The behemoth that encompasses the prison is called by many names. The most meaningful ones, I think, are those that convey the pervasiveness of its power: the way it infects the world outside as well as the people within.

Scholar and activist Beth Richie uses the term "prison nation," describing it as "a broad notion of using the arm of the law to control people, especially people who are disadvantaged and come from disadvantaged communities."[2] That control can take the form of prisons, jails, surveillance, policing, detention, probation, harsh restrictions on child guardianship, the militarization of schools, and other strategies of isolation and disposal particularly deployed against poor communities of color, especially black communities.

Others have used "prison nation" simply to demonstrate the system's vastness—how it infiltrates our culture and fuels our national politics, often in invisible ways. "Prison-industrial complex" (PIC) is another key term; Rachel Herzing of the prison abolitionist group Critical Resistance defines it as "the symbiotic relationship between public and private interests that employ imprisonment, policing, surveillance, the courts, and their attendant cultural apparatuses as a means of maintaining social, economic, and political inequities." The concept emphasizes how financial and political powers use prison and punishment to maintain oppression, making it look natural and necessary. Prison doesn't stop at the barbed wire fence, and it doesn't end on a release date.

Ninety-five percent of prisoners are released. They're emerging from their isolation poorer and more alienated than when they went in. They're coming out with fewer economic opportunities and fewer human connections on the outside. Some come home to find that "home" no longer exists. Many, like Kayla, fall into harmful patterns, sometimes in order to survive, sometimes because they feel they have nothing much to live for. Others are reincarcerated for the flimsiest of reasons as "parole violators," especially if they're black or brown or Native or gender-nonconforming or poor. More than 40 percent of those released return to prison within three years.[3]

Isolation does not "rehabilitate" people. Disappearance does not deter harm. And prison does not keep us safe.

We Can Do Better

A society built on the principles of freedom and shared humanity is possible. In fact, its seeds have already been planted, and they are growing every day. The second half of this book looks at what people are doing right now to dismantle the prison nation and deal with problems—both individual harm-doing and larger social wrongs—through connection rather than isolation.

All over the country, people are implementing community-based accountability and transformative justice strategies, making human connection both their jumping-off point and their objective. They're cultivating environments—classrooms, neighborhood programs, workplaces, homes—that foster antiracist, anticlassist, pro-humanity approaches to justice. They're combining new models of doing justice with larger movements for change, taking on the deep structural issues that drive the current system.

Overcoming imprisonment isn't just about climbing out of "the Hole." It's about collectively imagining and creating the culture in which we want to live, once we reach the surface. What follows is a portrait of a society coming apart—and some glimmerings of ways we can begin to come together.

Part One

Coming Apart

Chapter 1

The Visiting Room

Loneliness gnaws at the essence of who we were. The hunger for
connection with the outside world is what, in the end, turns us
callous, creating delusions that we are better off lonely.
—*Abraham Macías,* * Pelican Bay Prison*

When my parents and I visit Cook County Jail for the first time
in February 2009, it is a Saturday and the place is jam-packed. We
squeeze into the slow-snaking security line, which curves around
several ropes and bumps up against the doorway. Some visitors
stare at their feet, hands stuffed in their pockets, trudging forward
every few minutes when the line loosens. Others shout to their
children to stay within the roped boundaries, fearing that they'll
be booted out for causing a disturbance. A thin, shivering woman
standing in front of us is shaking her head over and over, rocking
a blanket-covered baby in her arms.

As we inch closer to the metal detector, a guard pulls a tall
young woman off to the side, gesturing to her short skirt and
scoffing, "You think you can come in here like that? Huh?" After a few hesitant protests—"Sorry, sorry, I didn't know"—she
walks away slowly, toward the exit, face in her hands. We follow
commands, removing our shoes and socks, stepping through the

metal detector, raising our arms for the pat-down, following the officer who escorts us across the yard.

After a three-hour wait, we're called into the visiting room, and we file through the narrow door. It's a short, dim corridor lined with wobbly stools facing a thick wall of plexiglass with several barred holes. On the other side of the plexiglass, Kayla shuffles in with a few other women. They scrunch down in a row, each opposite their visitors, and lean toward the holes. We start talking—well, screaming—back and forth. We don't scream because we're fraught with emotion, though we are. We scream because we can't be heard otherwise, due to the thickness of the plexiglass divide and the compressed cacophony of the fellow visitor-screamers competing with us on either side.

Eventually, I just go for it and press my mouth up against the bars of the hole so Kayla can hear me. I taste sweat and sour steel.

"How's it going?" I scream.

"It sucks, what do you think?" Kayla shouts back. "I feel like my life is over. But, at least, I'm working out." She twirls, her dismal blue smock flaring wearily.

Kayla's arms have grown quite muscley (push-ups are a favorite pastime in jail), and her eyebrows are meticulously groomed, if a little greasy.

"Your eyebrows look awesome!" I yell.

"Thanks—we did them with thread that we pulled out of our jumpsuits!" she yells. "They don't let us have tweezers! I learned it in Audy Home." The "Audy Home" is the old name of Chicago's juvenile detention center, where Kayla spent some time in 2005 and 2006. Now she pauses, then knocks her head lightly against the plexiglass, her eyes closed. "But no one gives a shit about my eyebrows, if you think about it. I just don't know what else to do."

Mom and Dad take turns. Then I'm back on the stool. We

quickly run out of things to talk about: Kayla doesn't want to belabor how hopeless and miserable she's feeling, and I don't want to carry on about the happy things in my life—or the frustrating things in my life, most of which seem ridiculously trivial given the circumstances. Later, my dad observes, "What's left to scream?"

Soon, a jarringly loud buzzer sounds, silencing all conversation. A guard calls time: Our thirty minutes are up. Kayla and her companions rise to march out. "I miss you I miss you I miss you I love you…" Kayla calls, the ends of her words quivering. She touches her fingertips to the plexiglass before she's led away. Then, "TIME!" a guard barks on our side of the glass, and we fall in line, too.

They Make Life Matter

The visits my parents and I pay to Kayla in jail are accompanied by a constant mantra that pulses through all of our minds: *This is temporary.* We're white, we're middle class; my sister and I grew up in a neighborhood where few people had ever been in prison. Kayla's sentence is not long. Our privilege affords us the opportunity to frame imprisonment—the first time around—as a bad dream. Regardless of how relieved we are that Kayla has been incarcerated, that she's off the street and probably sober, implicit in the relief is always the notion that this saga will come to a close, that "real life" will return, even if it doesn't last.

For a whole lot of other visitors, trips to prison are infused with a more painful pulse. This act of visiting is the real life of their relationship. It lives this way over the course of many years and, sometimes, forever. And so my visits to Kayla are laced with thoughts of the families I've come to know through my interviews, families whose bonds are maintained—and often lost— through bars.

One prisoner's familial situation has permanently set up residence in my mind by the time Kayla is incarcerated. She is Danielle Metz, a California prisoner and mother of two who's been separated from her children for most of their lives. I first wrote to Danielle in 2007. I was plugging away on a couple of long feature articles about federal prisoners serving life sentences, and was knee-deep in bland, evasive statements from members of Congress, most of whom didn't intend to lift a pinky to contest the harsh policies in place. Danielle's lucid honesty shone through the murk. She was serving three life sentences plus twenty years for a cocaine "conspiracy" conviction. (Her husband was a high-trafficking dealer.) Danielle was locked up in Dublin, California, more than two thousand miles from New Orleans—her home, and the home of her parents and two kids. Citing racism (she's black), poverty, negligent public defenders, and unjust sentencing practices, Danielle expressed little hope for a commutation of her sentence, barring a pardon from the president.

"My story is like a lot of stories you see, but can't really put a face on," she wrote me. "In communities where I'm from, this type of thing happens all the time." It's true: One in 40 American kids has a parent in prison, and for black kids, it's 1 in 15.[1] Increasingly, those parents are mothers; women are the fastest-growing group in prison.

No matter what problem we were discussing—federal parole, the pardon system, prison conditions, useless lawyers, useless laws—Danielle's letters wandered back to the topic of her children. She was grappling with a stark, practically unanswerable question: How do you parent from prison? It's a question most prisoners are asking themselves, since a considerable majority of them have kids who are minors.[2] Danielle responded to it with a quiet verb: "watching."

"It hurts to watch your children grow up from 3 years old and 7 years old to 22 and 19," she wrote. "Years ago my children used to be so hopeful that things would change. Then [I was] seeing them evolve into adults right before my eyes. Seeing them eager to come visit, then not wanting to see me because they say it hurts too much for them to come year after year and see me in prison."

After reading her letter, I sent myself a short, scrambled email:

The Point:
Family, loved ones, community!
—love, support (hopefully)
—They make life matter

"They make life matter" has stuck with me. Prisoners frequently tell me there's "no point anymore," that incarceration has extinguished much of their will to live. Most say that—more than the cramped and dirty quarters, the harsh treatment, the lack of sunlight, the baloney sandwiches—this sense of pointlessness stems from their frustration and sadness about the people they've lost, the ties that have dissolved over time and distance. Many prisoners also mourn ties that were broken already, and they now see an even slimmer chance of healing. Others mourn the bonds that never existed in the first place; prison has laminated and preserved their isolation. Where is life in its "mattering," for prisoners watching their outside relationships erode and their possibilities for new bonds wane, watching the months drift forward and the chasms grow wider?

The Modern Slave Auction Block

The "chasms" and "distances" are more than metaphors. Jeremy Travis, a leading prisoner-reentry scholar, calls the prison-industrial complex "a modern version of the slave auction block."[3] Upon the strike of a gavel, people who've been convicted may be bussed to far-off prisons, hundreds or even thousands of miles from their families—most of whom are poor and can't afford to travel far or often to visit them. The metaphor is all the more apt because a large proportion of those families are black. As chronicled in Michelle Alexander's *The New Jim Crow*, national incarceration rates are a product of the prison nation's groundings in slavery and ongoing anti-blackness. African Americans are currently about six times as likely to be incarcerated as whites, and therefore six times as likely to be uprooted from their families and communities.[4]

Abraham A. Macías Jr., who cracks me up on first contact by referring to his lockup at the notorious California supermax prison Pelican Bay as a "vacation" at "Pelican Bay Resort and Spa," describes how his incarceration 750 miles from his hometown has unraveled his familial ties. "Stuck way up at the California/Oregon border, in the middle of nowhere, seems to erase you from the world," says Abraham, who's originally from East Los Angeles. He says he can't blame his family for not visiting more frequently. "It's the cost of gas, taking days off from work, the 36-hour round trip, 18 hours to and from … and for what?" he says. "Three hours behind a glass window talking over a phone?"

For some prisoners' families with whom I've spoken, their loved one's transfer to a far-off prison has meant, flat-out, the end of visits: The money just isn't there. In 2004 (the most recent data at this writing), more than half of state prisoners and a little less than half of federal prisoners said their minor children had never visited them.[5]

More and more families are finding themselves in this position: In the past couple of decades, out-of-state transfers of prisoners have soared. As prison populations have ballooned, many states have dealt with overcrowding by shipping people off to prisons across state lines.[6] Even prisons within state lines tend to be plopped down in the middle of abandoned fields or former factories (generally, in depressed rural areas where land is cheap).[7] Prisoner placement "procedures" run something like, "You go here, you go there": Primary considerations include security level (minimum, medium, maximum) and the availability of open beds, not prisoners' proximity to home.

Some weak rumblings toward addressing the problem of distance have surfaced recently: Select prisons in at least twenty states have implemented "virtual visits," using video conferencing. It's a hopeful prospect for some families who can't make the trip, but for many it manifests as a less-than-wonderful reality. Some jurisdictions charge bloated fees for each "visit"—in Virginia, folks on the outside pay $15 for a half-hour video chat, $30 for an hour[8]—and some prisons are actually cutting out contact visits in favor of video chats.[9]

Abraham points out that distance and cost aren't the only reasons family members don't make the trek. His dad, who died suddenly of a heart attack last year, once told him that he never visited because he didn't want to see his son "caged like an animal." Even if your loved one is incarcerated right across the street, "visiting" serves as a weak substitute for existing in the world as humans together.

"Visitor-Friendly"

For April Anderson, who was fourteen years old when her dad, Joe, was sentenced to life on methamphetamine conspiracy charges, much of life has centered around the visiting room for the past eighteen years. She's traveled to see him in prisons in five different states. It's carved into her family's existence, she says, as much a fixture as mealtimes and laundry: the four-hour (or more) drive to the prison, the humiliating security checks, the unfinished emotional business that trails behind them as they walk away. "For us, a family vacation basically means traveling to prison to see Dad," April writes to me in an email. "Conversations are not private but shared with the next inmate who is sitting within a few feet of you on either side. Armed guards and cameras are watching and capturing every word and movement. That's where all of our family photos have been taken for the past 18 years, with Dad wearing a hideous jumpsuit and all of us doing our best to smile."

Even after seventeen years, April and her family never know what to expect upon arrival at prison. "Rules" change rapidly, depending on the guard on duty. April's grandmother, Sue, tells me of an instance in which the two of them were kicked out after April hugged her dad and was accused of being "too affectionate with her father." Harsh, denigrating words are to be expected. This is common: When I ask prisoners' family members about the physical experience of visiting, they often use the word "punishment." Inside the walls, they're treated like prisoners themselves, particularly if they're people of color and therefore already classified as "dangerous." They're subject to invasive body frisks, rude or abusive treatment, and sometimes sexual harassment.[10]

Waiting rooms and visiting rooms are often dirty. Many don't offer seats or bathrooms, regardless of how long the wait may be. Sometimes the wait is many hours long. Plus, visitors can be turned away for anything from wearing the wrong clothes to popping up positive on an inaccurate drug hand-scan.[11] In at least one state—privatization-happy Arizona—visits are growing even more prohibitive for poor families: A mandatory $25 "background-check fee" must be forked over before visiting a state prisoner.

Though visitation is a frail substitute for a solid presence in community and family life, recent studies have shown that even these brief moments of contact contribute to reducing recidivism. (Reducing recidivism isn't the only way—or even the best way—to measure "success" in the system, but it is practically the only indicator that's measured.) A study out of the Minnesota Department of Corrections concludes that making visitation policies more "visitor-friendly" could result in "public safety benefits": More human contact, the logic goes, strengthens bonds that discourage reoffense and encourage positive behaviors upon release, which means a better life for former prisoners and safer lives for everyone else, too.[12] Even the federal Bureau of Prisons agrees, stating that visits, phone privileges, and mail service are provided because "research has shown that prisoners who maintain ties with their families have reduced recidivism rates."[13] This correlation illustrates the necessity of more "friendly" visitation policies—but the fact that more human contact means less recidivism begs some larger questions: What are the collective consequences of pulling people away from the people they care about in the first place? How does it keep us safe?

A Side Note: Wait, What About Conjugal Visits?

Questions about the purpose of physical separation take on a particular significance when it comes to romantic relationships. In the movie *Office Space*, unhappy cubicle-ite Peter Gibbons reassures a friend with whom he's planning an elaborate quick-money scam that even if they land in jail, it won't be so bad—in fact, it could be awesome. "The worst they would ever do is put you, for a couple of months, into a white-collar, minimum-security resort," he scoffs. "Shit, we should be so lucky! Do you know they have conjugal visits there?"

"Conjugal visits" are in fact banned almost everywhere and for almost all prisoners. Four states (California, New York, New Mexico, and Washington) allow a limited number of "extended family visits": time that can be spent in a more private setting, with either a legal spouse or other family members. (A few prisons in an additional four states allow overnight visits with children or grandchildren.) Though restrictions vary among different states and prisons, these choice visits are most often available to minimum- to medium-security prisoners who are STD-free and HIV-free, with no disciplinary markups while in prison. So where did Peter from *Office Space* get the idea that anonymous women might be magically carted in to satisfy prisoners' "conjugal" needs?

The concept of the conjugal visit was constructed explicitly on the foundation of controlling black sexuality. It originated in early-twentieth-century Mississippi, at Parchman Farm, a slave-plantation-turned-prison. The visits were introduced as a management tool intended to promote docility,[14] and were allowed mostly for black male prisoners, who were said to have an "insatiable sexual appetite" that might morph into violence if left unfed—plus, the thinking went, it would motivate them to work harder in the cotton fields.[15] The women involved were often sex workers brought in specifically for the purpose of quelling potential inmate "aggression." Conjugal visits began to spread across the country—they were considered an incentive to work and a means to "reduce homosexual behavior."[16] (The practice of bringing in sex workers was phased out in favor of spousal visits.) But in 1974, the Supreme Court ruled that these types of visits were *not* a constitutional right,[17] and amid widespread overcrowding and budget-tightening, programs allowing "conjugal" contact with spouses or partners have since fizzled to barely existent status.

Conjugal visits are, then, a pop culture–hyped yet near-mythical prison "perk." More common is the visiting room, a heavily regulated space, with the distance between participants measured and monitored. Joe Jackson, April Anderson's dad, describes the visits he received early on in his sentence from his then-wife, to whom he'd been married for seventeen years upon entering prison: "When she came to visit I could kiss her 'briefly' upon exiting. We couldn't sit by each other or even hold hands." Like much of the visiting life, the brief arrival of a partner is—on both sides—often simply a wrenching reminder of absence and loss.

"Water-Cooler Talk"

"Absence makes the heart grow colder, not fonder," Marcos Gray, an Illinois prisoner, tells me. He, like many of my pen pals, says he understands why his loved ones have stopped visiting. With every year that slips away, friends and family members become more "accustomed" to the fact that he's not there. They settle into their own ever-evolving lives that don't include him.

Incarcerated at sixteen on a sentence of life without parole, Marcos (who's thirty-six at the time of this writing) has spent more birthdays in prison than out. Nowadays, when the date swings around, he often doesn't receive a card, let alone an in-person greeting. He seems to have resigned himself to this lonely reality.

"We all would like to believe that we're irreplaceable to our loved ones," Marcos writes, leaving the second half of that thought (*but maybe we're not?*) glaringly unspoken. There's a difference, he says, between family members "wishing" that their incarcerated relatives would come home, and actually working to hold together the bond—a bond that, ultimately, can't help being strained, worn down, fractured. Many loved ones simply opt for the dreamier and more distant route: the "wishing."

Marcos's family ties didn't vanish all at once, he writes: "The strain came gradually and was so subtle that to this day, I still wonder what has happened." Weekly visits turned to monthly visits, monthly to quarterly. These days, only a few family members—his mother and two of his nine siblings—make an appearance. He says he's grateful for how long his connections lasted: Older prisoners had warned him that loved ones might slip away more quickly. "I'm lucky to have received at least a good 11- or 12-year demonstration of support from my family," he writes.

Abraham has a similar attitude: "outside" people's lives move forward, and in some ways they can't help leaving their incarcerated family members behind. Like Marcos, Abraham was incarcerated as a teenager. Neither feels as if his own life ever really "started" before it was stopped.

"As time steadily marches on into eternity, they have all marched on with their own lives: growing up, having babies, maturing," Abraham writes of his relatives and friends. "All the while, I'm here, stagnant in life experience, only knowing adulthood from within a prison cell." He's happy to have a "few diehards" who drop by once in a while, but he says that the visits tend to disintegrate into awkward "water-cooler talk." Conversation topics run dry fast when one participant's life feels so stuck and so estranged.

Lawson Strickland, who has spent the past twenty years incarcerated in the Louisiana State Penitentiary at Angola—a notorious prison built on a former slave plantation, where the primarily black prisoners still pick cotton—describes the state of incarceration as being "held outside of time itself ... a sort of stasis, akin to being trapped in amber." Lawson served seven years on death row and has since remained in semi-solitary confinement. He describes his isolation as not only a geographical separation but a temporal one: He resides, he tells me, "outside the flow of history."

Reading Lawson's letter, I think to myself: What do *I* talk about with people here on the outside, when we're getting together just to talk—that is, when we're "visiting"? Usually, we're telling each other our ongoing histories, the events and the choices, the slippery path forks that we navigate to pave the timelines of our lives. Nonprison "visits" with people we haven't seen for awhile—say, a family reunion, or a week's stay with an out-of-town friend—are usually occasions for updates: relationships, births, deaths, bankruptcies, graduations, trips, breakups, new homes, new careers, new adventures, lost jobs, adventures cut short. But most of those milestones, even the horrid ones, are out of reach for prisoners, "trapped" in space and time.

As my dad noted back at Cook County Jail, after a half-hour of shouting to my sister through the plexiglass, "What's left to scream?" Lingering between the words of these "water-cooler" conversations is a sinking reality: Even for the most dutiful visitors and most appreciative visitees, prison feels like abandonment.

What does the feeling of abandonment do to people? What does the act of "abandoning" do to those who must walk away at the end of a visit? And if relationships are what make life matter—and, therefore, what spark people to change their lives—then what kind of change is generated by reducing prisoners' relationships to half-hour-long chats about eyebrow-threading … for them, and for us, and for the progress of our communities, our country, and our world?

"It's So Weird—She Just Stays Here"

When my parents and my partner, Ryan, and I visit Kayla at Decatur Correctional Center (a central Illinois prison) in early summer of 2012—she's in for retail theft, stealing over-the-counter medications to sell in order to pay for under-the-counter heroin—the four-hour drive there is, oddly, tinged with an upbeat air. It's a day trip with a mission. We ride into town: small, nondescript, somewhat decrepit houses wearing front-stoop flags, a cat sauntering here and there, a sign plastered with Decatur's town motto, "We like it here." The city's main claim to fame is that Abraham Lincoln lived there briefly circa 1830, and we glimpse a couple of standard-looking presidential monuments, boring ghosts perched atop flat green park lawns.

We stop in at a diner whose storefront sign proclaims it "best in town!" for midday omelets and piles of hash browns. On our way out, my dad pauses at the counter and asks a waitress for directions to the prison. The customer seated at the counter across from the waitress looks stricken, then looks down, swerving his chair a bit.

"I'm not *sure*," says the waitress, and goes silent. She moves away and begins slicing intently into a pie, as if Dad has burst out with a huge official secret, à la the emperor's new clothes. Perhaps he has. As is the case in most prison towns, the prisoners aren't local, and the prison, though it employs many of the town's residents, is still viewed as an imported incongruity.

The section of the prison siphoned off for visitors vaguely resembles the diner—bland outside, disinterested service staff inside—minus the omelets and kitschy posters. Decatur is a minimum-security women's prison. Unlike Cook County Jail, there are no long, cramped lines punctuated by guards barking orders. The waiting room is quiet and barely populated; family visits are much less frequent here. The four of us are privileged to be able to take the day off and spend the money to travel to this far-off spot.

A correctional officer (CO) leads us silently through a heavy door into a hallway, and my mother and I are intercepted by a female CO and pulled into a narrow, dusty room that smells like Lysol. Ryan and my dad are pulled into another. We're patted down firmly, and I flinch as the CO's hands pass over my breasts and between my legs. This is a mild ordeal compared to the strip search that prisoners themselves must undergo prior to each visit.

Inside the visiting room, the incarcerated women, all garbed in baggy, pale blue uniforms, are nevertheless dressed for the occasion: fingernails freshly lacquered in bright pinks and greens, just-applied layers of lip gloss and eyeliner. Later in an interview, activist and former prisoner Kathy Kelly tells me of how women hand over their meager dollars to the commissary (the prison store, which sells a rotating stock of overpriced items) for makeup and hair supplies, prepping compulsively for the visits of their partners, family, or friends. When Kathy first went to prison in 1988, the commissary sold only things like "oatmeal and Cracker Jacks," but the selection has ballooned along with the size of the prison-industrial complex, feeding off prisoners' desperation. Unable to control any other circumstances, many long to know that when family and friends catch a glimpse of them, they'll think, "At least she's looking good!"

Unlike Cook County's heavy-aired, crowded cavern with its shouting-through-the-glass misery, Decatur's visiting area is a real room, in which one can move one's arms and legs and even walk around. We hug Kayla, sit down with her at a small, round table, and watch babies play with their incarcerated moms, although, of course, that scene is not uniformly cheery. When conversation stagnates, we can stroll over (without my sister, who must stay seated) to the vending machine and purchase aged treats: Kayla has come to favor a stale-tasting peanut butter and marshmallow lump, the offspring of a Moon Pie and a hardened Twinkie.

"You would love it here, My," Kayla jokes, catching hold of my hand, swinging it back and forth. "No real meat. Soy sausage, soy bacon, soy hot dogs. It's like a really gross vegetarian restaurant." (I've been a vegetarian since the age of seventeen, a choice with which Kayla has never quite sympathized.) Decatur's nickname is the "Soybean Capital of the World"—though I feel like there must be other cities that claim that title—and the prison makes expedient use of the cheap and bountiful local crop.

I'm happy to be able spend an hour with Kayla face-to-face. But the relative "comforts" of visiting the prison bring to mind the fact that, unlike jail, this place is—for many of its inhabitants—a very long-term residence, very far from home. And despite her soy dog jokes and vending machine enthusiasm, Kayla's face is damp, stained with the residue of tears and sweat. She's shaking like crazy and explains that she's been sedated on large doses of prescription meds dubiously assigned for "anxiety," then abruptly pulled off of them. Our chatter is peppered with "um's." We revolve around safe topics, reaching for hypothetical fun activities we can do after she's out, which mostly just involve hanging out in public. Ryan and I share plans for our upcoming wedding, for which Kayla has a slew of ideas—purple candles, a rhinestone headband, a cheesy love song we both adored as kids. We nod and laugh and emit meaningless witticisms that skirt the fact that Kayla won't be there for the wedding, that she'll be here, crossing off the wedding day's box on her countdown calendar, probably crying.

Undergirding our visit is a sense of quiet desperation. We know Kayla has practically nothing to do all day besides paint her nails with polish purchased off the commissary. We know she encounters regular violence and degradation from guards.

We know that the drug treatment program in which she was enrolled upon entering prison has since been eliminated due to state budget woes, and Kayla, by her own admission, spends a fair amount of her ample free time yearning for crack and heroin. We also know this: Though Kayla will be released in six months, she has absolutely no postrelease plans. *How could she have plans?* I wonder. In prison, "outside" exists as a diaphanous dream; untouchable, it's sometimes tough to comprehend that it really still exists.

As we slip out, walking backward and waving to Kayla until the door shuts, Mom says, "It's so weird that now she just stays here." I look at her, then around to the other tables, where other prisoners' families are hugging and sobbing and leaving. "It's just a room, like any other room," Mom says. "It's almost as if she could just walk out with us!"

But of course she can't. We spun plenty of vague dream-plans for our future life together as we sat around that table. (Traveling to New York to see Grandpa! Playing basketball with Ryan! Finally meeting each other's friends! Writing together! Thinking together! Being "real sisters"!) But later that year, a couple of days after Kayla's release, the two of us are "visiting"—joylessly munching cookies at a coffee shop and talking about nothing. She looks up at me and shakes her head languidly. "I don't know what to do," she says. "I don't know what to say to people here. The only thing I know how to do is be in prison."

Chapter 2

The 100-Year Communication Rewind

It's been awhile. We've missed you!
—*Securus, Illinois' prison phone company, in an email I received
three months after Kayla's release from prison*

From time to time, Kayla asks me to send one of her incarcerated friends a card or a letter for a birthday, or a death in the family, or simply "so she can hear her name" called out when the mail comes around, to provide a brief interruption in the insular monotony of the daily routine. "Mail call" can be the pinnacle of the day in prison—or the low point, for those prisoners who don't receive anything.

When Kayla's locked up again in the fall of 2011, I don't pay her any visits: I'm living across the country in California, where Ryan is finishing his master's degree. I'm bored there—it's a small university town with little to do outside of academia—and spend most of my nonworking time pacing through the public library and wandering up and down the same streets. Maybe it is my loneliness, or maybe it's Kayla's desperation—but for whatever reason, over these months, we grow closer than we've been in years. We're linked almost solely by letters. We share our weirdest hopes for the future (I'm briefly obsessed with moving to the North Pole), our tiniest short-term goals (she is working hard to befriend a squirrel she has met in the yard), and her day-to-day activities (memorizing all the muscles in the human body, painting and repainting her nails).

Kayla apologizes for letting me down in the past. I apologize for passive-aggressively slipping off the face of her planet when I'm mad at her. In our letters, we tell each other the truth. (She says she's scared she'll never get clean.) My first words aren't "Where are you now?" and my last words aren't "Where are you going?" like they were when she contacted me on the outside. She reassures me about my (undoubtedly smaller) worries and woes. She calls me her best friend, saying, "You're the only friend who I've kept—or who has kept me." And at the end of that stint in jail, a small, selfish corner of me is sad to see her released—thrown back into a universe without moorings, where the promises, ponderings, hopes, and truths that livened the pages of our letters will likely be crumpled up and tossed in the free-world trash.

This, however, is not the usual story of mail call. Most prisoners' siblings aren't wandering around Davis, California, with an abundance of free time, a love of letter-writing, and lots of spare change for stamps. Abraham Macías—who's on year eighteen of a twenty-five-year sentence at Pelican Bay, in California—tells me that, like visits, his mail quantity dropped off fairly rapidly after a short time in prison. Most people don't understand how much it means to prisoners to receive a letter, he says, because in the "real" world it's not a valued commodity. Even his mom writes only sporadically.

"She'll send a book of stamps or a package of writing materials, with an apology for not writing. The way most people do," he writes to me. "Instead of writing, people send money, offer things on a postcard shout-out. They don't know what a simple note does for us in prison."

The absence of mail can also have direct bodily consequences. Rev. Jason Lydon, who runs the queer anti-prison group and pen pal project Black and Pink, tells me that for more vulnerable prisoners (these usually include queer and gender-nonconforming people), a lack of mail can mark a prisoner as alone, abandoned by folks on the outside—and therefore an easier target for harm, especially from guards. "Mail call happens in a public space, and so folks are hearing the names of people who are getting letters, day after day," Jason, who's been incarcerated himself—in a segregated unit for LGBTQ prisoners where guard-perpetrated sexual violence was rampant—tells me. "If you're not receiving mail for years, you're more likely to experience harm or violence, because they know that it's less likely there will be consequences, that there's no one looking out for you."

The ABCs of Mail Call

Mail is scarce for almost everyone in prison. One reason is quite basic: Many prisoners and their families struggle to—or flat-out can't—read or write. Among prisoners themselves, only 3 percent were classified as "proficient" in reading and writing in a National Center for Education Statistics literacy assessment in 2003.[1]

Lacino Hamilton, who's incarcerated in New Haven, Michigan, staring down a life sentence, points out that in Detroit, where he's from, nearly half of adults are considered "functionally illiterate."[2] "Not only are prisoners overrepresented in those horrific numbers, but so are the family and friends of prisoners," he says, explaining that many of his own kin fall into this group. "I often go months without family and friend contact." Black and Latino family members living in poor communities with fewer literacy resources and more barriers to literacy are disproportionately affected by the problem.[3]

The literacy barrier poses problems for another giant group: Many of the 1.7 million children with parents in prison simply haven't learned to write yet.[4] Pennsylvania prisoner Sable Sade Kolstee's three kids were all under the age of five when she was incarcerated, and for much of her three-year stretch of prison time, her only contact was a smattering of brief phone calls with her oldest daughter. Letters being impossible, she missed out on the nuances of her kids' development, their emerging personalities, their daily passages of thoughts and feelings. (First words don't translate very well to thirdhand letters penned by adult relatives.) As Sable prepares for a much-anticipated visit with her children, she writes letters to me, sharing her worries that her two younger kids "wouldn't know me and would be scared."

"Anything Can Happen to Prison Mail"

Even for prisoners who write up a storm, including the many with whom I've corresponded, the prison mail system can prove a formidable opponent to sustained, meaningful correspondence.

In early 2008, I was writing to Eugene Fischer, who was serving a life sentence for marijuana smuggling. (Since he was a federal prisoner, Eugene was ineligible for parole—though years later, in 2012, he was granted a rare resentencing and released.) At one point, I expressed frustration about the fact that one of Eugene's letters, which he'd referenced repeatedly in a later note, never made it to my box. Eugene, having had twenty years of prison experience to cushion the blow, took the loss in stride. "Anything can happen to prison mail, both incoming and outgoing," he wrote to me. Other prisoners and ex-prisoners have described this phenomenon—how there's virtually no accountability for their letters. Given that for many, it's their main form of communication, this unpredictability can contribute to their sense of helplessness, isolation, and bitterness toward the system.

Since prisoners' mail is subject to being read by staff, self-censorship is rule number one for ensuring that a letter reaches its destination. Prison officials in most states are permitted to peruse prisoners' mail at will,[5] so any letter written to or from prison has got to be composed for multiple audiences. (Kayla once said to me, "The COs really like your letters!") Each time I receive a letter, I wonder: which parts are really directed at me, and which parts are aimed at an anonymous third party dedicated to searching for what shouldn't be there, what words shouldn't be crossing the walls?

Beth Derenne, who co-coordinates the Women's Prison Book Project, is well schooled in the endeavor of getting not only letters, but *packages* (which are even more regulated and scrutinized) across those walls. I meet up with her in December 2012, at the small, independent Minneapolis bookstore where the project is based. The volunteer-run group collects and sends books to incarcerated women, corresponding with them about what books they'd like to receive. Beth regales me with stories of failed attempts to mail books; one can never tell whether or why a book will be sent back.

"A lot of prisons don't allow books that discuss sexual assault—so sometimes they'll even send back classic literature," Beth says, pointing to a copy of *The Color Purple* by Alice Walker. "This is crazy, because one fourth of incarcerated women have been sexually assaulted. But they can decide anything's a safety risk." She ticks off more rules from various prisons on her fingers: no LGBTQ-related books, no activity books, no Harlequin romance novels, no books involving witchcraft (including fiction).

Many of the books the women seek most are prohibited.

A few days later, Beth emails me a list that WPBP has compiled of restrictions at prisons around the country; regulations are always changing, so the project struggles to keep up. Limitations include "No blank journals," "no outdated magazines," and "no coloring books."

A 2011 report from the Texas Civil Rights Project notes that prisoners in that state are permitted to receive white supremacist texts like *Mein Kampf* and the *Aryan Youth Primer*, but can't receive some books by Henry Louis Gates, Sojourner Truth, Studs Terkel, Noam Chomsky, and Al Sharpton, on the pretext that materials containing racial slurs are prohibited—even if the "slurs" are included because they're being critiqued.[6] The report states, "The works of some of the finest African American authors, like Richard Wright and Langston Hughes, are banned for frank discussions of race. The context of these works, however, is irrelevant to TDCJ [Texas Department of Criminal Justice] censors." Also discussed is the banning of self-help books aimed at aiding survivors of sexual abuse in overcoming their trauma.

Sometimes, it seems, the censors just have a really bizarre sense of humor. The crowning rule on Beth's list: "No crochet books."

"Ah, the Phones ..."

With illiteracy, censorship, time, and effort making it tough to foster a sustainable relationship through the mail alone, phone calls are precious commodities. The first time Kayla called me from jail, I hung up two seconds in—right after hearing, "You have a collect call ..." (I was clueless, and missed the "... from an inmate at Cook County Jail; press five to accept the call.") Since then, my family and I have navigated an ongoing maze of different phone plans, call requirements, prepayments, and other hurdles in order to pay an absurdly large fee to a private company so we can talk to Kayla on the phone for a few minutes when she's in prison or jail.

This is the story of millions of prisoners' families' attempts at communication, except that many are halted halfway through: The costs are simply too high. Family members charged $1 per minute for a call may skip the call altogether, depending on their budget (which, considering the demographics of the prison population, is bound to be very tight). A December 2013 investigation by *Prison Legal News* disclosed some of the motives behind the prices of Inmate Calling Services (ICS), the prison phone company, whose rates

are much higher than non-prison rates, in large part because prison phone companies pay "commission" kickbacks to the corrections agencies with which they contract. Such commissions are usually based on a percentage of the revenue generated from prisoners' calls and have nothing to do with the actual cost of providing the phone service. Because ICS providers factor commission payments—which currently average 47.79% for state Departments of Corrections (DOCs)—into the phone rates they charge, the rates are artificially inflated.[7]

Recently, municipal governments in Chicago and elsewhere have started cracking down and cutting fees for jail calls.[8] The FCC has taken action to reduce the costs of calls across state lines, and some states have reduced their call fees as well. Still, almost every prisoner I've spoken with says that costs remain an obstacle for their loved ones.

No one knows the topography of the phone-rate battle better than New Haven, Connecticut, activist Barbara Fair, who regularly speaks out against the exorbitant fees. Barbara has seven sons (currently all in their thirties and forties), and all of them have been incarcerated at various times. Barbara has lived a breathless juggling act that revolves around the system and its barriers, paying weekly visits to multiple prisons, enduring panic attacks and sleepless nights, and working full time while taking care of the children still at home. The phone calls topped off the mountain of ever-renewing obligations: At one point, when three of her sons were in prison, Barbara's phone bill totaled out at $400 per month. She tells me that the pileup of fees "caused me to lose phone service many times, trying to stay on top of the monthly bills." This is an everyday occurrence in poor communities of color like Barbara's.

Even if the money's there, a relationship based on prison phone calls is an exercise in messy clairvoyance. The calls pop up unpredictably: prisoners don't know when they'll be able to use the phone, and for recipients, it's often not possible to pick up at the time the phone rings. Even for a work-from-home family member like me, the calls are easy to miss.

When you're able to catch one, it can be elating: your initial updates spilling out in a rush of pent-up energy, your loved one's voice audibly lifting at the sound of yours. My calls from Kayla have usually been peppered with frantic choruses of "I love you!" and condensed bursts of affection. "You mean so much to me!" "You're my best friend!" "You're *my* best friend!" "I miss you!" "I miss you more!"

Yet no matter how loving or deep your conversation, its parameters—and how little you control them—are never in question. Calls are interspersed with blaring notifications that you're on the phone with someone in prison. ("Ah, the phones," writes Abraham Macías, "with their constant interruption that reminds you and your loved one that they are on the phone with a 'California inmate'!") And they're cut off with barely a warning, often leaving you feeling further apart than you felt before picking up the call.

No One at the Other End

Prisoners quickly learn that even when they've surmounted the barriers of cost and restrictions, they still may not be able to make a call—at the drop of a plate, guards can yank phone privileges. David Martinez,* serving a life sentence in Florida, described one such situation: "There was a fight in another unit, nothing to do with the rest of the compound, and the warden decided to lock us all back down," he wrote me, a few years back. "[The warden] calls all the shots. The complex warden has taken our telephone, kept us on lockdown in our rooms for 24 hours, 7 days a week." Kayla has experienced the same thing to a lesser degree. Often, when we don't hear from her while she's in prison, it's because of a lockdown spurred by an isolated incident. Wardens may restrict telephone rights (as well as visitation) at will—there are no hearings or trials or appeals when it comes to disciplinary action inside the walls. When someone "acts up"—an action whose definition is usually at the often racist, homophobic, transphobic, politically repressive discretion of the officers—phone privileges are frequently the first to go.

All barriers aside, there's a nearly insurmountable reason why some prisoners don't make phone calls: There's no one left to dial. Mauricio Rueben, a federal prisoner serving a decades-long drug sentence in Texas, ticks off his lost calls in years. His wife of seventeen years divorced him eight and a half years into his incarceration, so that connection dropped off the wires. After ten years, Mauricio says, the "out of sight, out of mind effect" set in, and friends stopped answering his phone calls. After fifteen years, letters went unanswered, and the only way to contact anyone was by calling persistently. Twenty years in, he says, there's no one left but his mother and two brothers—and he doesn't call them often. "When I do call home … I can sense my family's hurt and discomfort of me being in here and they not being able to do anything about it," Mauricio writes to me, adding that a necessary "state of numbness" has conquered both ends of the line. "They are willing to end the call as soon as possible [rather] than to deal with these hard feelings."

Abraham Macías talks of fellow prisoners who have phone privileges, but no one to call. "There are guys in here that haven't had a phone call in 20 years," he says. In order to reach out, prisoners must retain some vestige of connection with someone who'll accept the call on the other end. They must be able to identify specific people on the outside who are still in their lives—people with whom the ties are strong enough, the relationship copacetic enough, and the money, well, *there* enough to pick up the phone. An endeavor to reach out to new people on the outside—to cast out a line into the unseen larger world—can become a monumental quest. The line has simply gone dead.

"How Do I Compete with Facebook?"

Ironically, over the past thirty years' incarceration boom, another boom has taken place—in communication technology. The world has exploded with a dizzying swarm of new ways to connect. Yet for many who are locked up, the prison door feels even more tightly shut. It's a murky equation: Society has evolved to a place where, no matter how far you are from home, you can connect with your loved ones in seconds—if you've got the resources. But in order to maintain the prison—an institution that not only isolates, but also *subtracts* people from society—prisoners must be not only removed from their communities but also cut off from the maze of intricate networks by which contemporary humans exchange information and emotion.

And so, while many on the outside move on from letters and phone calls to social media, email, Skype, texts, and whatever comes next, some incarcerated people still can't get their hands on an electronic typewriter. Kayla talks about prisoners who haven't touched a computer—ever. Not all incarcerated people experience technological restrictions in the same way: Federal prisoners and a slowly growing number of state prisoners are able to receive (and sometimes send) emails, for a fee. Like phone services, these limited email systems are operated by private companies and are subject to close surveillance.[9] Access to the Internet itself—beyond email—is prohibited.

The ban makes intergenerational contact especially tricky. "Having a teenage daughter ... how do I compete with texting, Facebook and Twitter?" Abraham writes to me. He now hears from his daughter three or four times per year. "I write in hopes to develop some kind of relationship, but I can't compete with the instant reply that kids are used to these days. The only thing to do is hope my daughter reads my letters and knows my love for her is unconditional." Abraham acknowledges that aside from his daughter, an Internet connection wouldn't improve his family relations: Most of his relatives don't have regular access to a computer.

To be sure, efforts that strain at the seams of this disconnect have existed and evolved since the dawn of the Internet: Many prisoners' families and outside allies have started up blogs, websites, and Facebook accounts in their names to rally support for them and to give their words an audience. A few sites publish prisoners' blogs for a broader readership, including Between the Bars, where any prisoner can send entries to be scanned or transcribed and posted, and the Sylvia Rivera Law Project's blog, which regularly shares uncensored posts sent in by members of the project's Prisoner Advisory Committee. These types of outlets provide incarcerated people with vital ties to the networked world. Still, they must depend on prison postal mail and the gatekeepers that process it to bring their words to the web.

When I ask Alex Friedmann, the managing editor of *Prison Legal News* and associate director of the Human Rights Defense Center, for the forecast regarding the ongoing Internet ban, he doesn't predict any changes on the horizon. Alex, who spent ten years in prison and jail himself before his careers in journalism and activism, rattles off a list of logical explanations. "The purported reason is due to security; prison officials don't want prisoners googling 'improvised prison weapons' or 'how to escape in five easy steps,' or bringing up the blueprints from the prison where they're confined," Alex says. "Other concerns involve searching for contact info to intimidate or threaten witnesses, or coordinate gang activity or other illicit acts via the Internet. More likely, though, is that prison officials don't want prisoners to be viewing porn sites." Is this deprivation simply about punishment, or does it aim to restrict specific thoughts and behaviors, stultifying the possibilities of fantasy-based, "virtual" sexual connection, just as physical connections with those outside are severed?

Whatever the rationale, the prospect of Internet access does seem a precarious business: Inching open the door to the web could diminish and demystify the prison walls. At a time when much of social life takes place virtually, access to those channels might swing open the gates of interaction in a way that the early prison architects could never have dreamed possible. Thus, to solidify the inside/outside barriers that define and maintain the institution of prison, the Internet ban must live on. And, according to Alex, it's not fading away "anytime soon."

Bleak Offerings

As a person who works remotely and spends most of my waking hours online in some capacity, it's hard to envision a tech-free life. So, in the fall of 2012, as Kayla's release from prison draws near, I'm convinced that a successful adjustment to the online universe will ease her acclimation to the rest of it. I crouch over my computer late at night, allaying my insomnia by setting up brand-new Gmail and Facebook accounts for Kayla: fresh accounts for a fresh start. I decide that, as a nice little surprise, I'll scope out her Facebook social scene and send some requests, so that upon her reinauguration into the free world, she'll have more than zero "friends."

I "suggest" friendships with some of her old pals, and with some of my longtime buddies whom she vaguely knows and probably remembers. Then I glance through the profiles of her friends who've done prison time, or are currently serving time. It's eerie: Their Facebook walls have morphed into memorials. They're scattered with wishes of "love" and "hope" and "courage," sent out into the ether, as if they'll fly beyond the screen and alight inside the prisoner's cell. The posts are bleak offerings, withered testaments to the connections cut short by incarceration.

To call prison "isolation"—and to leave it at that—wouldn't be quite accurate. It's more like this: Prison seals its inhabitants off from the world, and then sells (by means of visits, or commissary products, or phone calls, or stamps, or email) a stunted version of the world back to them, in bits and pieces. Sometimes, links to the world are sold for money, sometimes for compliance, sometimes for racial privilege, sometimes for political docility, sometimes for gender normativity, sometimes for luck.

It's like wrapping someone's head in airtight plastic wrap, then offering to sell them measured sips of oxygen, a little at a time, for years on end. Once those years pass, will that person remember how to breathe naturally, as second nature? And even if they've never had the luxury of breathing naturally—if their lives have always been suffocated in one way or another—will their months or years of systematic, supervised suffocation really teach them how to breathe free?

Chapter 3

On the Homefront

I remember Judge McBryde saying "life," and Mom screaming over and over, "You can't do that! You're not God! You can't take someone's life."

—*Billy Jackson, son of federal prisoner Joe Jackson*

In the classic game Monopoly, the square called "Jail" sits ominously in a corner of the board. It's a hole into which an unsuspecting player might fall after an unlucky roll of the die, or the drawing of a bad card, or simply stumbling upon a space marked "GO TO JAIL" while ambling along the path to riches or ruin. Once you've been "sentenced," you've got just three possible routes out of your lonesome confinement: luck (rolling doubles), privilege (a Get Out of Jail Free card), or money.

But once in a while, players stuck inside the jail square have company. A pale green space clings to its outward-facing perimeter: a kind of dry, liminal moat between Jail and the edge of the board, inscribed with the words, "Just Visiting." A player who happens upon Jail without being mandated there isn't punished, but must merely spend a brief turn in the square, then get along on her way to other squares and other ventures, as if it had never happened.

However, in real life the vision of prison isn't over for family members after they exit the visiting room, or hang up the phone, or put the letter back in its envelope. The fact of a loved one's incarceration can take on a vacuous life of its own, rambling along invisibly, parallel to yours, inhabiting your sleep, your daydreams, and your minute-to-minute fears and imaginings. It's sometimes difficult to whisk your mind back to your own reality and live visibly in the present while they are—as Wisconsin prisoner Miguel Segarra puts it in a letter—"stuck in the past."

"Life Has Never Been the Same"

In talking to families of incarcerated people—and then trying to write about them—a hard-to-shake anxiety tugs at my brain and my fingertips: "What's the *ending*?" One author I spoke with when I began working on this book advised me, "Keep in mind that you're writing a book for Americans, and Americans like a happy ending…. Or, at least, a hopeful ending." But for a lot of people embroiled in the system, there's no narrative arc, no reassurance of a liberated tomorrow. The very nature of incarceration ordains an impediment to forward movement—and that impediment is frustratingly vivid to family members on the outside, who witness the rest of the world rushing forward firsthand.

This dissonance bubbles to the surface when I speak with Yvonne, ex-wife of Joe Jackson, a pen pal of mine who is serving life for a meth distribution scheme undertaken to raise the $250,000 to pay for his son Cole's life-saving bone marrow transplant. Joe divorced Yvonne three years into his imprisonment, telling her he wanted to set her free—but she still holds on. "They took the one person that had my back no matter what…. They took my best friend, and life has never been the same," she tells me. "We live in our own prison out here, one that never ends."

Joe has been in prison for more than eighteen years.

Joe's daughter, April, describes to me how the saga began, during an early-morning breakfast when she was in ninth grade. It was still dark outside, the house hushed, and she had just seated herself at the table to eat a bowl of cereal. Then came a blaring loudspeaker-voice from outside the front door: "Come out with your hands up!" April yelled for Yvonne, who lay asleep in her room with baby Cole; he slept curled up next to her so she could tend to the protruding catheter in his heart when he woke in the night.

There was no slowing down the SWAT team: Two hundred officers swarmed everywhere in the house, in the woods outside, all down the road. They burst through the doors, searching futilely for April's absent dad, tearing through papers and pulling Yvonne onto the porch. "One of them gripped me like a sack of potatoes and carried me to the driveway," she says. "They told me to shut the dog up or they would shoot him.... From that day forward, my kids have had a fear that someone was watching them, and they all slept with me til they were older. It takes away all the security in your own home."

In this small Texas town of fewer than 1,500 people, the scandal was big news. Rumors took flight immediately ... and they never quite landed. "I learned we had elevators leading to an underground drug lab with an elaborate network of tunnels that went from our home down to my grandmother's.... Trust me, I would have found that had it ever existed," April recounts, recalling some of the worst items of gossip. "Apparently, there were also four dead bodies uncovered in our backyard."

At the age of fourteen—for many of us, the height of caring what people think—April watched as long-standing friendships evaporated within days. Parents barred their kids from coming over to her house, and some even told their children not to talk to April or her middle brother, Billy. Yvonne got the cold eye, too—fellow parents wouldn't sit next to her at the kids' basketball games, and she was voted off the PTA in a closed-door meeting. She says, "There was rumors about me and the kids, always."

The word "stigma" originally referred to a brand, a mark burned into human skin with a hot iron, commonly imprinted on the skin of enslaved people or "criminals."[1] The word hasn't evolved much in the 400 or so years since its first usage, though the mark is now social instead of physical. And in the current era, at least when it comes to incarceration, the "branding" can be contagious, smudging off on families in ways that shift both their public image and their personal sense of self.

"The Bills Never Stopped"

Joe Jackson was handed the maximum possible sentence for his offense: three "lifetimes," plus an extra thirty years piled on top. As they wobbled back into their own lives after the sentencing, Yvonne, April, and her two little brothers struggled for footing. Financially, things were a mess.

It's not like the Jacksons had been living large in past years; April grew up in a trailer for the first ten years of her life, and says, "Dad barely made enough to get by." But Joe's imprisonment threw the family into a deeper, shakier pit of financial unpredictability. Their car was repossessed, Cole's medical bills piled up to the ceiling, and Yvonne waged a constant battle to keep their house while working overtime at multiple jobs: a deli, house cleaning, construction. "Joe made our living so I could take care of Cole," Yvonne says. "Without him it was me trying, and some days the bills never stopped."

It's a common turn of events: While prisoners are "stuck in the past," family members are often left floundering to make up lost income. Most incarcerated parents were employed prior to their arrest, according to a 2005 study by the Urban Institute.[2] (And that doesn't count money the incarcerated person was bringing in by "illegitimate" means—also often used to put food on the table.) Sometimes, the family has lost its only income source and must start from scratch.

Amid money troubles and the strain of separation, family tension continued to tighten for the Jacksons. Yvonne and Joe divorced, with Joe insisting that it wasn't fair for him to keep Yvonne tethered to him while he waited out the long years to die in prison. April pulled away from her mom, and, desperately seeking closeness, plummeted into a relationship with a controlling boyfriend who rapidly turned abusive. It took two and a half years to disentangle herself.

Meanwhile, April's brother Billy slid toward violence himself. Crushed and confused by the loss of his dad—and angered by his classmates' derision of his family—he got into frequent fights. Frantic at the possibility of another family member straying down a troubled path, Yvonne yanked him from school, homeschooling him on top of her other jobs (including, of course, caring for her chronically ill younger son).

Yvonne's concern was no delusion. Boys whose parents are incarcerated are five times more likely to become incarcerated themselves,[3] and kids of prisoners are more likely to go to prison than to graduate from high school.[4] The effects often hit early on: Between 30 and 50 percent of children placed in juvenile detention centers have at least one parent who's been to prison.[5] According to a report by The Sentencing Project, "The arrest and incarceration of parents ... takes an emotional toll on children, leaving some psychologically traumatized, fearful, anxious, withdrawn, socially isolated, grieving, or possibly acting out their feelings in disruptive ways."[6]

Of his dad's incarceration, Billy says, "I think it caused me to grow up way too fast. I was twelve when I started working full time, started dating a girl when I was fourteen and was married to her at nineteen. I never really had a chance to be a kid, so when I was twenty, I started acting like one, and got in a lot of trouble and pretty much lost everything, including my now ex-wife, by the time I was twenty-one." As for April, she fled her small town as soon as she could. These days, she completely avoids it. She doesn't want to respond to the persistent "how's your dad doing?" inquiry. It always has the same answer.

April hasn't given up hope, though: She channels her frustrated energy into fighting for her dad's release, applying for commutations, reaching out to public figures, connecting with activists. Meanwhile, Joe mails me a family picture taken on July 14, 2013. Like every photo for the past eighteen years, it's set in a visiting room. Joe's in his prison khakis, flanked by his children, including Cole, who, thanks to his lifesaving transplant, is alive, healthy, and smiling at twenty-three. A city skyline—a faux backdrop made available for visiting-room snapshots—sparkles behind the huddled group. "If I didn't have my family, I'd just curl up and go to the next level," Joe writes, signing off with his usual closing: "Your friend in a cage."

Moving Out, Punching Holes

Even after years of hearing family members' stories of loss and disconnection, each one still pricks me with weird surprise. I'm surprised to be surprised: Most of my brain, of course, knows way too well that incarceration has reverberating effects, hitting and marking all sorts of other people besides those in prison themselves. But a part of my mind still inhabits the pervasive, official logic of the prison-industrial complex, and that logic is all about subtraction. Prison's role in society, the logic goes, is to toss away the bad eggs so they can't poison us—so we don't even have to see them. With those eggs cleared, we seamlessly close up the gaps and carry on, clean and whole.

The surprise pops up when the broken seams are revealed— the way that incarceration rips open new holes in the social fabric of families and communities outside, severing intricate networks strung together in ways that are observable only upon their breaking. Instead of eggs, we are tossing away people's mothers, fathers, daughters, sons, brothers, sisters, partners, friends.

Those split ties are concentrated heavily in poor communities of color. While the fragmentation of black families (especially the departure of fathers) has, in dominant political and cultural spheres, often been attributed to personal failings, Michelle Alexander points out, "Hundreds of thousands of black men are unable to be good fathers for their children, not because of a lack of commitment or desire but because they are warehoused in prison, locked in cages."[7]

When a loved one is locked up, those left behind are often less able to participate actively in community life and in the economy, strained by severe shortages of money and time. There are sometimes more subjective forces tugging them away from their communities, too: shame (on their end) and fear or suspicion (on their neighbors' side of the fence).[8] Families' self-isolation is compounded by the fact that some of their neighbors—such as Yvonne's fellow basketball parents inching away from her on the bleachers—aren't crazy about seeing them, anyway.

Often, family members relocate out of their communities either upon incarceration (in search of more affordable housing, since they've lost an income-earner) or afterward (in hopes of a less stigma-tainted transition).[9] And as they walk away, they leave behind friends, schools, religious groups, and support networks—those ties that link families to the world.

In communities where incarceration is common, these ongoing removals, isolations, and relocations can prove a formidable barrier to building a stable, close community in which people know each other and look out for their neighbors. Researchers Todd Clear and Dina Rose, who have studied incarceration within the context of families and communities, write that the way in which imprisonment disrupts connections can actually make harm and conflict more likely. The researchers frame the effects of incarceration as a type of "social disorganization," a process that interrupts lives, shaking and scattering the collective life of a community. An important part of preventing violence, according to Clear and Rose, is maintaining "informal social controls": structures *besides* laws and law enforcement.[10] These are things like neighbor interaction, community groups, close friend networks, and peer pressure (the good kind!) from loved ones.

So, when lots of people are moving in and out of a neighborhood—or isolating themselves to the point that they may as well have moved out of the neighborhood—the effectiveness of those informal controls plummets. It's hard to maintain strong community networks if you're not even sure who's in your community. Add to that the fact that those who are incarcerated have themselves "moved out," abruptly and with no choice in the matter (Clear and Rose call this process "coercive mobility"), punching holes in the networks they left behind.[11] This phenomenon is deepest felt in poor communities of color, where high proportions of people are incarcerated.

Barbara Fair, the New Haven mother whose seven sons have all been incarcerated, hails from one such neighborhood. Unlike April Jackson's small-town "friends," many of Barbara's neighbors have provided empathy and support: "Going to prison ... was so common in my community that there wasn't much of a raised brow about that," she says. This commonality lends families in neighborhoods with high concentrations of former prisoners a unique base of communal support. If almost everyone has a relative or friend who's been incarcerated, they're less likely to judge.[12] But residents are so supportive, in part, because they know all too well the venomous power of the stigma that runs thick outside the bounds of their neighborhoods—a stigma that captures prisoners, their families, and their communities in its widening net, isolating them in a sort of external jail of their own, in which actual imprisonment seems devastatingly predestined. As legal scholar Dorothy Roberts puts it, "Because all of the children in these communities have some experience with prison and may expect to be behind bars at some point in their lives, prisons are part of the socialization process.... Incarceration is a 'rite of passage' imposed upon African American teenagers."[13]

A Landslide of Consequences

The criminal justice system has coursed through Barbara Fair's life for decades, starting when she was a teen and her brother was sentenced to prison. Soon after, Barbara herself was incarcerated for a couple of weeks—delivering a sharp premonition, she says, of emotions to come. She tells me, "I can still feel the pain and humiliation that cut through me." Barbara's kids grew up in the thick of the drug-war years and could serve as poster children for the strangling effects of that "war" on poor, black families. Each has been locked up for a drug-related conviction. "The greatest factor influencing my sons ending up in prison is the fact that they are young African American males, and thus the targeted commodity for the prison industry," she says.

Barbara explains that not only are black males a targeted commodity, they're an *assumed* commodity; they're viewed as suspicious from youth on up. Her words mirror an interview I did with Mariame Kaba, the founder of Chicago's Project NIA, an advocacy and education organization aimed at ending youth incarceration. Mariame spoke of how kids of color begin their lives weighed down by an obligation to prove their "innocence." Unlike their white counterparts, their "guilt" is presumed from the start. "Black and brown youth are born with criminality inscribed on them," Mariame said. "When they commit crimes, that's just confirmation. Their job is to prove they're *not* criminal." On top of this assumption of criminality, family members of prisoners are often handed a whopping serving of guilt-by-association. Siblings often have it the worst, according to Todd Clear, who interviewed a group of families in an impoverished, mostly black neighborhood in Miami. In *Imprisoning Communities*, he writes, "Siblings often bear the brunt because there is the idea that if your sibling could be a criminal, then you could too."[14]

As her sons were carted off, Barbara's life quickly molded itself around prison and its immediate effects: the weekly visits to various facilities—each at least forty-five minutes from home—the expensive phone calls, the panic attacks, the money troubles, the time constraints, the sadness.

Even after her sons came home, she wrestled with the lingering reverberations of their imprisonment. By the time Barbara and I get to know each other in 2013, all of her sons have been released, but her youngest—deeply traumatized by his time behind bars, some of which was spent in isolation—currently lives in a psych ward and still depends on his mother for constant support.

Barbara's ordeal is just one example of how the incarceration of large numbers of men (especially black men) generates a landslide of consequences for women. In an interview, gender and criminology scholar Beth Richie tells me, "Clearly one of the 'untold stories' of mass incarceration is the way that women are disadvantaged. The most obvious part is their own incarceration. But ... there is also the problem of women supporting men who are incarcerated and when they are released. It is visiting, housing, feeding, protecting, hiding, taking the rap for them. All kinds of things have women 'working' to create or maintain stability when men are incarcerated, or when [their] kids are incarcerated."

Barbara Fair carried on this support work routine, sevenfold. But amid the sleepless chaos, she gleaned a panoramic view of the system in which she was entangled—and became convinced that the best way to cope was to dig in and fight it. In the years since, Barbara has jumped into the struggle full-force, traveling the country to speak out about bail, plea bargains, sentencing, juvenile justice, and the war on drugs. She's reached out to Yale students to collaborate on projects like "The Worst of the Worst," a video aimed at exposing the harmful effects of solitary confinement. She led a fight to oust a corrupt New Haven judge, she held a "Biking While Black" protest to speak out about the anti-black profiling of bikers on the street, and nowadays she's working to set up dialogues throughout Connecticut between victims and people who've caused harm.

Yet after thirty years, the challenges are still just beginning, says Barbara. She's thinking long-term—and big: "I have worked so hard at reform, and saw so little change, that I have come to the conclusion that revolution might be the only response to what is occurring in America relative to criminal justice and the prison industry it feeds."

The Incarceration Wish

At this point, I need to acknowledge an uncomfortable but prevalent conundrum: Occasionally, a family member's incarceration has its perks. For some families, the prisoner in question has posed a real threat in their lives. Most victims of domestic violence don't call the cops—often because they know that police involvement would make their situations worse, especially if they're people of color.[15] Still, one-half of stalking instances, one-fifth of intimate partner rapes, and one-quarter of intimate partner physical assaults *are* reported to police, according to the US Department of Justice's most recent survey.[16] Police intervention and incarceration may seem, for the folks who've been harmed, a chance to cut ties and build a safer life.

It's not a lasting "solution," of course; the person is almost always eventually released from prison. And the incarceration of the family member (and the loss of their income) often creates fresh problems. In fact, many victims become direct targets of state violence upon reporting harm by their partners, especially if they've attempted to defend themselves physically, and particularly if they are black or brown.

Beth Richie notes, "Black women who report male violence to state officials are more likely to encounter uninformed service providers, unsympathetic community members, and rigid representatives of the state who blame them for their experiences and ignore the structural preconditions that surround them and their families."[17] Still, in the prison nation, incarceration is presented as the official go-to means to separate people from those who have harmed them.

Likewise, families of people with addictions have been taught by decades of drug war policy to see incarceration as one of the few surefire means of separating their loved ones from their substance of choice. Even those family members who recognize that continued drug use in prison is sometimes possible tend to feel reassured. For the chunk of time in which an addict is locked up, loved ones may breathe a little freer. They may let go of a bit of that clinging terror that their daughter or son or sister or aunt or brother or uncle or father or mother might be sprawled on a street somewhere, unconscious, ticking away the lonely minutes until death.

Kayla's friend Jake, incarcerated at the time he writes to me, acknowledges that his mother has mixed feelings about his incarceration. "One thing I know for sure," he writes, "is that she can sleep at night now while I'm in here because she knows where I am. She knows I am 'safe,' or safer than I was while I was out in my madness where there was no telling if I was dead or alive for weeks at a time."

What *exactly* are we wishing for when we want someone close to us incarcerated? Maybe this question can only be answered with further questions, in this system mired in confusion and propelled by fear. Here are a few: Do we want them to stop hurting us? Do we feel prison would keep them safer? Do we want to freeze their spiraling criminal record, before they get in even *worse* trouble? Are we so angry at them that we just want them to go away for a while, reassuringly immobilized on the corner of the Monopoly board? Or do we feel that, when it comes down to it, clamped down under the force of the prison nation, there is just no other way?

Come October 2012, my family is tossing around these questions on an hourly basis. There's absolutely no danger that Kayla will physically harm us. But we can answer a weak and weary "yes" to at least a couple of the other questions. Four days after Kayla gets out of prison—two days after telling me that all she knows how to do is be incarcerated, one day after I proudly presented her with her brand-new Facebook profile—my mother finds her passed out on the bathroom floor, a needle stuck in her arm. A chilling and tear-ridden trip to the hospital follows.

Two days later, an old boyfriend of Kayla's, newly released from prison himself after doing time for residential burglary, has crept into my parents' house during the night to bring her heroin. My dad, jolted from sleep, slides open Kayla's closet door to discover this man standing there, silent but barely shaken. "Hi, Mr. Schenwar," Kayla's ex-boyfriend says.

My dad can't coax his body back to sleep that night, or the next, or the next. Dad is prone to cyclical, major depression, but at the time of Kayla's release, he's staved it off for twelve years, climbing to a rare point of joy and calm. The rest of us remark that he's "enlightened." But now he's scared—for Kayla and for the family—and he paces the house, shaky and sleepless, sinking back into depression.

Kayla is scared, too. In a wild, honest instant, she thrusts a bag of heroin into my mom's hands and says, "Take it. I don't want it in the house." My parents, flustered, discard Kayla's advice to flush it, since they don't want it traveling into the water supply; instead, my dad, gingerly clutching the bag, walks it over to the police station. The amount of heroin is minuscule—it's about a fifth of what a typical addict might use in a day—and after my dad conveys his circumstances, the police say nothing. Dad may have been the first person ever to appear in their station, unsummoned, to surrender a bag of heroin. Still, I wonder how their response would have differed had Dad been black.

A week later, my parents, Kayla, and I meet at a café for a disastrously executed half-intervention. It ends with me screaming maniacally, "Fucking asshole! You're ruining everything! Do you want to go back to prison? FINE! I never want to see you again!" Her limp, teary reply floods out before my rant is through: "Fine, bitch. I never want to see you, either!" We exit before we're banished, the other café-goers' eyes escorting us out the door. Leaning against my car in the café parking lot, Kayla and I half-hug and concede grumblingly that we love each other. Neither of us indicates that we actually do want to see each other again.

We talk soon after, though. Her calls come at dawn or late at night, wrenching me from sleep, and they're always the same: Each conversation balances itself on a thread of watery banter, sometimes toppling into hopelessness before one of us slams down the phone. At home with my parents, the fights are constant. Kayla's days are containers of empty hours; her job searches crumple on the spot. There's no way to cover up the three-year gap in her résumé where jail and prison have carved a gulf in her work life, and background checks ensure that she doesn't have a decent shot at even the jobs for which she's qualified.

On Christmas Eve, two and a half months into her parole, Kayla's hauled off to jail for retail theft. She calls my mom, then me, with the news. Number one: She's been arrested, and once she's sentenced, she'll more than likely end up back in the penitentiary. Number two: Her post-arrest urine sample has revealed some unexpected information—she's pregnant. Number three: Can one of us please post bail?

I talk to my mom, then my dad, then Ryan. Bailing Kayla out seems like a $500-steep exercise in pointlessness. She may get rearrested, and soon. (Her bond is $5,000, which means $500 must be paid to get her out on bail. Bail keeps you out of county jail while you're awaiting sentencing—but, of course, that's moot if you get picked up again.) Besides, we have reached the end of our collective ropes. We don't *want* her out. We don't want to pace our kitchens agonizing over her whereabouts, wondering if she's dead or dying; anticipating another near-overdose, another offense, another strike on her record, another trip to the joint. We sigh into the phone, reciting the events of the past two and a half months to each other, again and again, as if, this time around, we'll "solve" them. We don't post bail.

Chapter 4

"Only Her First Bid"

I've got the prison thing down pat. I can get by in here. I'm not ready to die out there.

—*Kayla, spring of 2013*

Eventually, some friends of Kayla's do put up the $500 to get her out, and we return to a stasis of daily unpredictability. I check my phone compulsively, always anticipating word of a new arrest. The winter wears on, and I offer Kayla limp, token gestures of concern. I ask around about jobs at local restaurants, pick up some papers for her at the methadone clinic, say, "You can do it!" As I say this, I'm not exactly sure what "it" means.

We meet for lunch in late March, three months since she was last in jail, five months until the birth of her baby. Kayla moves and speaks—when she speaks—with an undercurrent of hopeless nausea. When I ask how things are going, she says "horrible." I toss out a feeble comment about how the pizza place down the street has tacked up a "We're Hiring" sign. Kayla nods and makes a note on her hand. She's probably indulging me. A couple of weeks ago, she applied for a job at a home supply store, and they loved her and told her she had it, and then they did a background check. Bam. Of course, the odds were not in her favor. Recent Illinois statistics aren't available, but in New York, 70 percent of parolees are not employed.[1]

All of a sudden, Kayla looks straight at me. "The day before I got out, when we got our 'reentry orientation,' they brought in these old inmates to tell us how they succeeded after prison," she says. "They were saying things like 'Now I make $90k a year and have five acres,' and 'Now I've got three kids and run my own business.' They should've brought people in who said, 'I got out and couldn't find any work, ever,' or 'I work three jobs but they pay so bad that I can't support myself let alone my kids.'" She glances down at her lap and says to her chewed-to-blood finger-nails, "I miss prison."

The next day, she calls me, half-crying, half-screaming, so loudly I must hold the phone at arm's length: "What do I do? What do I do? ANY SUGGESTIONS?" The words scrape jag-gedly in my ear, echoing themselves sickly. *Do about what? The baby? The joblessness? The future, as an ex-felon?*

"What do I do?" As the days pass, Kayla begins to quietly an-swer her own question. She disappears for long stretches, fading out through my parents' door in the early afternoons, resurfac-ing days later, flopping into bed and slamming the door. "I got things to do," she mumbles at the floor, when asked. Amid the disappearances and the mysterious "things," the fights and the midnight phone calls, we find out that her baby is due September 3. Her name, Kayla announces in a brief moment of utter, serene sobriety, will be Angelica.

In late May 2013, when Kayla's sentenced to a year in the penitentiary—during which time she'll give birth to her baby—I barely remember which "thing" she is being sentenced for.

"No One Would Buy Those Cars"

Kayla once told me that, during the beginning weeks of her first prison sentence, when she slipped up on an obscure rule in her kitchen job, guards would comment, "She'll learn—it's only her first bid!" The assumption that there'd probably be a second bid (prison slang for "sentence") always hung in the air. Disheartening as their comments may have been, those guards knew the drill: Many of Kayla's fellow prisoners at the time were in on a second, third, or fourth bid. Each bid, it seemed, had ushered in the next, making prison a little more "normal" each time.

The magnetic pull that reels Kayla back to incarceration, again and again, is hardly unique: More than 4 out of 10 ex-prisoners return to prison within three years.[2] Many more come close: A recent Bureau of Justice Statistics study showed that within that three-year timeframe, 67.8 percent of released prisoners were re-arrested.[3] While some recently released prisoners are arrested for new offenses, others are reincarcerated for violating the conditions of parole, which may impose curfews, restrict whom the parolee can associate with, or confine where they can live or work. A failed drug test is a sure-bet violation.

At one point, I ask Kayla whether her parole officer provides any support in her job search or her quest to get sober. She laughs a little and says that, when it comes down to it, there's one main point to his job: to "violate" her if she messes up. Soon after, my mother, attempting a last-ditch effort to engage the court system in getting Kayla on track, asks Kayla's parole officer whether the state might be able to help find her a rehab placement. "Nope," he says. "But what I can do is violate her. Do you want me to do that?"

Decisions about whether to "violate" a parolee are largely up to the discretion of the officer, which leaves a wide, unchecked field open for racist determinations. A 2009 Colorado study showed that black parolees were eight times more likely to have their parole revoked by the parole board than their white peers.[4] The study's author, Professor Sarah Steen, noted, "We feel confident in saying that race seems to be an important factor in parole revocation decision making." And so, for a huge number of prisoners, the door out of prison is a revolving one.

Looking at the rate at which released prisoners are sent back to prison isn't an ideal way to gauge the "success" of the system. It would be better determined by whether those being released are able to build fulfilling, happy, well-fed, healthy, well-housed lives that contribute to the good of humanity, liberated from both official and unofficial forms of oppression—including targeting by police. But recidivism rates are really the only widespread quantitative data we have on the topic, and they do tell us something about whether people released from prison have shifted out of the circumstances that got them locked up. Alex Friedmann, my pal at *Prison Legal News*, points out that looking at recidivism is important because it measures whether the "justice" system is accomplishing its own stated goals. The main stated goal: preventing people from doing the things that led to their incarceration.

Alex's verdict on how the system is faring at its own game? "If a company produced cars and 43 percent of them were defective, the company would go out of business," he tells me, alluding to one of the most conservative reincarceration estimates, from the Pew Center on the States.[5] "No one would buy those cars. But that's how we operate our criminal justice system."

What does that mean for those of us on the outside? Let's consider another number: Ninety-five percent of prisoners will, at some point, be released. If prison makes us feel more secure because it disappears the "troublemakers" from our midst, what does it do for us if those of them who've committed harmful acts in the first place are likely to continue doing so once they reappear? If my sister's ex-boyfriend, incarcerated for residential burglary, is breaking through my parents' window upon his release, what does that say about that feeling of security? Upon checking her ex-boyfriend's record in June 2013, I discover he's now in the county jail, awaiting sentencing on a theft charge ... and he's been incarcerated for robbery, burglary, and battery at various times throughout the past sixteen years. Once he's sentenced and spends yet another two or three or four years isolated from society, what are the chances this man will emerge "reformed"—less prone to heroin use and more employable?

Mainstream social scientists are now hypothesizing that, at a certain point, incarceration actually promotes crime.[6] Large-scale studies from the Justice Department have linked high rates of incarceration with high rates of reoffending, and recent data shows a correlation between reduced crime and reduced prison populations.[7]

As early as the 1970s, officials were decrying the failures of mass incarceration to improve "public safety." The US government–sponsored National Advisory Commission on Criminal Justice Standards and Goals reported that prisons were, essentially, useful only for confining people who were serially prone to extreme physical violence. In fact, just a few years before the war on drugs began to blow the prison population up to five times its size, the commission recommended that no new prisons for adults be built and that juvenile facilities be swiftly shut down. "The prison, the reformatory, and the jail have achieved only a shocking level of failure," it concluded.[8]

After one has passed through this rite of failure, what comes next—or what's supposed to come next? "Reentry" is the most common term for the process of a prisoner returning to society. I'm not crazy about it. What are prisoners "reentering" into? What were the circumstances they left behind when they went to prison—and when they leave prison, who's to say those circumstances have changed? For many, the reality becomes a circular rotation through the innards of an omnipresent system, from which an exit—let alone a "reentry"—feels nearly impossible.

"It's Healthier to Disconnect"

Mauricio Rueben has "*only* two more years!" on his thirty-year marijuana-trafficking sentence in federal prison. In a letter to Eric Holder (a copy of which he sends me), he writes, "I am a black male, born in Cuba, raised in Texas, been in the US my entire life. I paid my taxes, received my voters card, registered with the US military, and was summoned for the occasional jury duty." After twenty-eight years in prison, he strains to continue to feel a part of the society to which he pledged loyalty, the society he left behind half a lifetime ago.

He tells me: "The truth is that anyone sentenced to over five years will have to undergo some degree of disconnect in order to mentally survive on the inside. Not hearing from friends and loved ones, not being able to do anything about anything that happens to sons, daughters, mothers, brothers etc. is emotionally, mentally, and physically stressful. If one dwells on the outside events, it can wreak havoc on one's health. Thus, it is healthier to disconnect to some degree."

This psychological switch is hard to flick off upon release, he says, and he points to it as an important factor that functions alongside more visible oppressions, helping to explain why the same faces keep popping up in prison as the years pass. "I've seen many men come, go, and come back again. Most of them on a violation, but a fair share on a new case with double-digit sentences," Mauricio writes to me. Lots of them, he says, emerge to find that the mental "disconnect" that served them well in prison deals a blow to their ability to survive outside.

Inside prison, one's most evident identity becomes "inmate," as opposed to partner or parent or child or grandchild or friend. By the time of release, that "inmate" identity—the person distanced from family, whose contribution is "unnecessary," who does things wrong, whose abandonment is preordained—can cling to a person. According to a study headed by Todd Clear and Dina Rose, the researchers who described imprisonment in terms of "social disorganization," prisoners tend to self-isolate once released: "We saw evidence of isolation when we asked returning offenders about their neighbors; frequently they said they were careful to stay away from people, and claimed not to know the neighbors."[9]

After incarceration, many of the mechanisms that help keep people accountable for their actions—ties with family, ties with community—are frazzled and misplaced. Former prisoners often return to homes that are either gone or no longer theirs, families that have either dispersed or grown to tolerate their absence, neighbors who may fear or stigmatize them, and a society that marks them as "offenders" and doesn't let them forget it. On top of that, they're usually heading back to hard-hit neighborhoods, mostly poor communities of color, where many, many people's lives and homes are regularly interrupted by incarceration, making it even more difficult to establish lasting networks that foster accountability.

The "Strong Walls" and the Cagers

The idea of the "deterrent" potential of isolation has long been subject to skepticism. In 1898, following two years of incarceration for "gross indecency" (that is, sleeping with other men), the playwright Oscar Wilde endeavored to distill the ethos of imprisonment in his poem "The Ballad of Reading Gaol." On its surface, the poem chronicles the story of a murderer being hauled off to his execution, but it is haunted by a larger message:

> I know not whether Laws be right,
> Or whether Laws be wrong;
> All that we know who lie in gaol
> Is that the wall is strong.

Wilde is saying that, for himself and his fellow prisoners, the desperation and anger sparked by confinement rise above all other responses to their environment. *The wall is strong.* An overwhelming reality dominates the world of prisoners: They can't get out.

But what about those tough-to-sort issues of "right" and "wrong"? What about prisoners coming to "know" the harm that they've inflicted on others (if they have indeed inflicted harm), coming to the realizations that'll help them avoid those actions in the future? It's a tough prospect in prison, says Lacino Hamilton, incarcerated in Michigan. He explains his thinking: "Those committing crimes over and over again … have not dealt with the void in their lives that leads to the act itself." In order to do harm, he notes, you usually have to be able to disregard the effects your actions have on other people. And imprisonment—a life in which isolation is constant—provides an atmosphere in which those effects on others can simply continue to be ignored or repressed.

Prison guards, who function as the human embodiments of Wilde's strong walls, are trained to constrain and suppress, to enforce zoo-like isolation. Guard-on-prisoner violence is routine, and, true to the undergirdings of the institution itself, is infused with racism, sexism, heterosexism, ableism, and transphobia.[10] This explicit violence often goes unrecorded—even unacknowledged. It is cleanly isolated and therefore easily suppressed; often, guards need merely close a cell door and walk away. Although the US Supreme Court held in 1993 that "an inmate has a constitutional right to be secure in her bodily integrity and free from attack by prison guards," the very structure of prisons—in which guards are explicitly handed the mission of controlling prisoners' bodies—belies that ideal.[11]

Rev. Jason Lydon, who founded the queer, antiracist prison abolitionist group Black and Pink after his own incarceration, describes how the act of sexual violence is built into the institution of prison, which cuts off from the rest of society not only your mind and words and thoughts, but also the solid fact of your body. "It's about restricting the body, controlling the body, so that other people have access to your skin anytime they choose," he tells me over the phone. "You have no right to say no." When Jason was incarcerated in Georgia, he was placed in a segregated block confined to gender-nonconforming and queer people. The experience played out as, in Jason's words, "torture":

Preachers would come into our cellblock on Sunday morning and tell us what abominations we were, and we were forced to stay in the room to listen to them. Prison guards would force us to strip naked in the dayroom in order to get our clothes, while all the other prisoners around in the other tiers would humiliate us. Strip searches are a form of sexual violence no matter what happens—but when I was further assaulted by a prison guard during a strip search, that really solidified in my deep self that this system causes so much harm.

One in five men experiences sexual abuse in prison; the estimates for women vary quite a bit, but reach one in four in maximum-security institutions.[12] (Such "abuse" doesn't include the lack of privacy prisoners experience while showering, changing, and on the toilet.) Lesbian, gay, bisexual, gender-nonconforming, and/or trans prisoners experience overwhelmingly higher rates of assault, often by authority figures.[13]

Jake Donaghy, a friend and fellow prisoner of Kayla's at Logan Correctional Center, writes to me about the ways that guards manipulate bodies into deeper isolation. Jake is transgender and describes how trans people are "kept safe" in the women's prison where he's incarcerated: "Say someone is trans, [and] fears for their life in any sort of way. They are placed in Segregation—'The Hole'—where one is confined to their cage for 24 hours a day and fed through a tiny window that is built into the steel door that can only be opened with a key." In a study of trans and intersex people in New York men's prisons, the Sylvia Rivera Law Project noted, "Interviewees report being subjected to disproportionate isolation and solitary confinement where they experience regular physical and sexual assault, harassment, and the denial of food and urgent medical care by correctional officers."[14]

Confinement in the Hole is also prison personnel's go-to response to those who break explicit rules (not just implicit ones like "don't be queer or trans"). Jake writes of the psychological and physical violence inflicted on prisoners: "What does that do but create more anger and resentment in an individual? In most cases, let's use mine for example—I know for a fact that I will walk out of these barbed wire gates more traumatized than I was when I entered them."

About a month after my sister's 2013 return to prison, I receive a letter from her that hits similar notes: "This place, this time down is turning me into someone I didn't ever want to be … mean and very hateful with a bitchy exterior," she writes. "You know that's never been me, Maya."

Christian peace activist Lee Griffith, who writes on the spiritual significance of this force-driven cager/caged relationship, notes, "The problem is that prisons are *identical in spirit* to the violence and murder they pretend to combat…. Whenever we cage people, we are in reality fueling and participating in the same spirit we claim to renounce."[15]

"Why Get Out?"

For people who are caged, the lighthouse twinkling in the distance may almost always be freedom—but "freedom" doesn't look the same for everyone. For those who anticipate a homecoming of homelessness and hunger, for example, the lighthouse twinkles less brightly. It also depends how deeply feelings of worthlessness and criminality have set in. It's possible to get used to anything, Oklahoma prisoner Gabrielle Stout writes, and for some, the anticipation of release mixes with a contradictory wish. After all, for many, going home resembles a different kind of incarceration— another arena of the prison nation, characterized by surveillance, racialized police targeting, and the crushing force of poverty.

Gabrielle has drifted between jail, prison, and the streets since the late 1990s, arrested on drug possession and theft charges. As both Native and transgender, she's a prime target for profiling, as well as for discrimination and abuse while incarcerated.[16] She writes to me of the harsh scrutiny to which she's subject as a trans prisoner—how she, like Jake, is prone to ending up in especially restrictive circumstances for relatively minor infractions: an unmade bed, talking across the unit, walking on the wrong side of the sidewalk in the yard. Over a year ago, she was placed in an intensive supervision unit, on twenty-three-hour lockdown. She is permitted one hour of recreation per day and three showers per week. Her mind has slipped into such a stupor, Gabrielle says—a state so different from that required to function in society—that often she's on autopilot. "I'm used to being in here," she says, "so why get out?" She's watched this shift play out in other prisoners as well. "You become so comfortable with the prison setting and lifestyle, that it's all you know," she says, noting that after a while, lost connections with people on the outside also begin to feel almost normal. "You don't feel like you would be able to make it if you were released."

Not long after Gabrielle's letter, I receive one from Kayla, in which she talks about her "comfort" in prison and fear of her out date several months down the line. At that point, not only will she be flung back into a world that doesn't want her, but she'll also be subject to a whole other round of severed connections; her closest friendships, at this point, are with people on the inside, many of whom won't be leaving for a long time. "Some of my best memories stem from inside these walls," she writes. "Although disturbing, it's my reality."

So I go to prisoners with a question that feels bizarre: Do they *want* to get out?

Most say they do, but they're scared. When I ask Sable Sade Kolstee, a former community college student from Pennsylvania and twenty-six-year-old mother of three young children, what frightens her about her impending release, she answers without hesitation, "My biggest fear is anxiety." This might seem tautological: Isn't fear anxiety? But, prisoners tell me, when you're relegated to an intensely dehumanizing state of confinement, unexposed to the daily interactions that outside life brings, it can be terrifying to imagine yourself immersed in a constantly flowing world of other human beings. Sable, who's kept to herself in prison, puts it like this: "Sometimes I think it will be over-stimulating when I can actually have contact again. We desensitize so much…. I know I will be nervous when I'm touched."

Pulled away from the people she loves, she says, she has become an expert at retreating into herself, faking invisibility. No one is demanding her presence; after all, severed personal connections also mean severed personal obligations. There are no kids tugging at her hands, no parental caretaking responsibilities to face. "Now, when confronted with an uncomfortable situation at times I look for the quickest way out, instead of working it out," she says. Later, after her release, Sable writes to me: "When I am in public, large crowds, I shake and nearly shut down…. It's like sensory overload and I have to have a timeout for three hours. It's frustrating because I want to be normal."

For prisoners incarcerated at a young age, the prospect of release looms especially intimidatingly. Abraham Macías, imprisoned since he was eighteen, is confined in the Secure Housing Unit (SHU) at California's Pelican Bay Prison. He lives alone in a cramped cell with no windows, a few pictures from magazines affixed to the wall, and a corner piled with manila envelopes stuffed with papers and photos, his only other possessions. To picture his living space, he says, "Get a TV, take it into the restroom, and lock yourself in. But you can't use the tub or shower. That's our existence." He and the seven others in his "pod" spend their limited yard time in a "23 x 5-foot concrete box," with a scant view of the sky that affords no sunlight for months at a time. It has been years, Abraham says, since he has seen the sun or the moon.

Abraham talks about life on the outside as a stack of faded memories, thin as dreams. And though he wishes fervently he were free, his before-prison life played out as a battle waged daily: His main concern, he says, was survival. With "friends getting gunned down" and "no food in the fridge (literally none)," he turned to "self-medicating" with drugs and alcohol, obtained through "illegal activities." He knows that upon release, most of his human interactions will probably revolve around the same make-ends-meet struggles. And he'll still confront racism-fueled police scrutiny. (Abraham is Latino.) "Brown and black men/women are mostly targeted in inner cities as suspicious characters, has-beens and any other name you can think of," he writes. He's seen fellow prisoners of color released, only to be rearrested almost immediately for small infractions. The idea of release is instinctively joyful, Abraham says, but in real terms, what—and who—will he be released *to*? As Gabrielle puts it, the question that pulses through her when she thinks of getting out isn't simply what she'll do—it's whether she'll be able to "make it."

And so, in this prison nation, release is a weighted "freedom." During the rise of the mid-twentieth-century civil rights movement, poet Gwendolyn Brooks wrote the poem "truth," about the complicated heaviness that may descend on someone emerging from the "night-years":

And if sun comes
How shall we greet him?
Shall we not dread him,
Shall we not fear him
After so lengthy a
Session with shade?

When the door is flung open, and access to the "sun" seems within reach, the path forward is not simple: A million barriers and cliffs lie beyond the doorstep. And for many prisoners, once the sun comes, it can feel blinding, with the instant pressure to "make it" in an oppressive world overwhelming the warmth of its rays.

"But He Had a Record..."

What does it mean to navigate the daylight—to "make it"? Is it to "rehabilitate"? To find or reignite companionship and love? To attain a joyful and fulfilling life? To avoid a return to prison? Or, simply, to survive?

I visit the Chicago office of US congressman Danny K. Davis for an interview in the spring, as Kayla's latest sentencing date draws close. Though many of his colleagues have only recently come around to the idea of scrutinizing criminal justice policy, Davis represents a district that houses some of Chicago's poorest neighborhoods—mostly black communities that have been torn and scattered by incarceration—and he has long advocated legislation addressing the rights of currently and formerly incarcerated people. I first met him in 2008 while writing a story about federal parole; parole has been abolished on the federal level since 1984, and the congressman had introduced a bill to reinstate it.

When I visit his office in 2013, he speaks of how, upon release, former prisoners remain isolated by labels. He speaks of a man who works for him, who was arrested as a juvenile for laughing at a police officer, "disturbing the peace." Later, as an adult, he attempted to become a police officer himself. He took the exam, passed, but was denied by the police board. Why? "He was a good person, an intelligent person, but he had a record," says Davis. Criminal records become former prisoners' badges of identification, the defining characteristic that tells the world what kind of human they are. One glance at the badge can mean being refused food stamps, or Pell Grants, or public housing, keeping lots of former prisoners separated from their families even upon release.[17] Many formerly incarcerated people already lack crucial job skills, since technology has evolved so rapidly over the past few years—some have never held a cell phone, others have seen the Internet only on TV. Prison also teaches patterns that are contrary to those needed for many jobs. Tack on the "convict" badge, and their chances are toast.

There are, of course, former prisoners who wear other badges. Some—mostly folks who had middle-class backgrounds upon entering prison—secure well-paying jobs and cultivate close relationships soon after release. Others emerge to become great poets, artists, and writers, having honed their craft while in prison. One such former prisoner, Joe Loya, found clarity and a love for words while incarcerated, wrote a beautiful memoir (about, in part, his years as a bank robber), and years after his release became a valued mentor for me during the writing of a difficult article. Many former prisoners become activist leaders, sparking change inside and outside of prison. (See Chapter 7 for more on this!)

But as Richard Shelton, a poet who ran workshops for thirty years in prisons, writes of prisoners' futures, "They get brutalized or they get butchered or they get out, but precious few of them … get out in a better condition than when they went in. Those few are the miracles."[18]

And if Sun Comes, How Shall We Greet Him?

In May 2013, Sable writes to tell me that she's preparing to leave her Pennsylvania prison. She feels thankful to be paroling to her grandmother's house, when she writes to me just before her release. But, she says, she's seen how poverty, disconnection from family, habits of hopelessness, and systemic unpreparedness have set up her fellow prisoners to fail when they are plopped back into the world:

> Some women have no place to go so they are released to a "center"—that is smack in the middle of drug grounds. If you walk out the door they can "cop" at the corner. The environment is not healthy to keep people clean.... They can't get a job.... Others make a choice not to care, not to try, and have reservations with their drug of choice before they leave. I see it every week. Women leaving just to come back.

A few weeks after her release, Sable writes me again, saying that although she's got a place to stay, "Job hunting is nil.... I had a plan for most things, but now that I'm home I see my plans don't really help. It's all in coping with the ever-changing environment." She's working hard to stay out—to build a life in the altered world she now faces—but that world doesn't know about the plans she's made, and it certainly doesn't bend to accommodate them.

Like Sable, Donna McDaniel, serving a thirty-year sentence in a federal prison in Texas, sees women leave "to come back"—that is, they're coming back on purpose. With no loved ones left and no roof over their heads, "the older women here that don't have family had rather stay right here. They get the medicine they need and three meals a day.... At least they won't have to pay those bills every month." Donna herself will be sixty-four years old upon release, and she is hazy on plans for post-prison living. She's in the process of connecting—and disconnecting—the dots on her waning constellation of remaining family ties, and she isn't sure who'll be there to support her. She has one son but doesn't harbor any illusions that he'll take her in; a couple of years ago, he simply stopped answering her calls.

Most prisoners depend on their families to help them pull through postrelease, both financially and emotionally. In an Urban Institute study, 71 percent of formerly incarcerated people cited family support as a key factor in helping them avoid a return to prison.[19] So those who "reenter" society without strong human connections are essentially deposited onto the edge of a cliff. Housing, food, health care, and the heavy labor of emotional readjustment can loom as insurmountable obstacles.

However, back in Chicago, Congressman Davis tells me that very often, the ultimate flashpoint—the "reentering" dealbreaker—is a job. Work means money, of course, but a job also does other things for a person. We reside in a world, unfortunately, where "What do you do?" means "How do you make money?" Employment means a channel into the sphere of the Doing. Since many parolees are jobless, work is yet another thing that chops off this group from the rest of society. And if they live—have always lived, maybe—in a situation where many people don't have work, or do work that's criminalized, the barriers can feel even more calcified. The road forward is narrowed to the point that a life without some supplementation that brings with it danger of future incarceration seems unattainable.

The fact that some kinds of work—sex work, for example—are outside the law should not denote that they are not valid, valuable forms of labor.[20] My objective in pointing to them here is to show the circularity of the current system: People are incarcerated for engaging in the informal or street economy, but upon release, the work available to them may well be limited to the informal economy. Tiffany, a pen pal of mine who grew up in Chicago but is now incarcerated in Georgia, talks about her fears of the complete lack of "legit" jobs available, and what that void may yield. "I don't want to be 'free' and broke," she writes, "cause to me that ain't living."

Though new policies prohibit employers from officially barring people with criminal records from applying for jobs, it's still tough to convince an employer that they should "take a chance" and hire you. Even employers in states with "ban the box" laws can still carry out background checks, and most will inquire about the inevitable gap in a formerly incarcerated person's work history. Congressman Davis tells me, "They never get to show who they are."

Harvey Fair, the brother of Barbara Fair (the New Haven activist whose seven sons were all incarcerated), talks with me over the phone about two and a half months after his release from prison. He's just spent seventeen years incarcerated for possessing a gun, thanks to a federal mandatory-minimum law that dictates that one spend at least fifteen years behind bars for gun possession if their records contain prior felonies. Harvey is black, a factor that renders him nearly twice as likely to be slapped with a mandatory minimum-carrying charge than a white person who has committed the same crime.[21] Now fifty-eight years old, Harvey has spent much of his middle age, as well as most of his twenty-year-old son's life, locked up. He's currently living at a halfway house in Florida and looking for a job—a tough prospect, given his "felon" badge and the gaping hole in his work history. He says of a recent job interview at an auto dealership, "I explained that I'd been incarcerated, and the guy literally started shaking."

When I ask Mauricio about his fellow prisoners who've been released recently, he writes to me with a tragic story:

A person I knew here that was released late last year, after twenty-one years in prison for bank robbery, was not able to cope with the environment of the halfway house and was sent to a hold-over [short-term prison facility] till March this year. After four months on the street, yesterday, he decided to rob another bank. After not being able to evade the police ... he pointed the gun to his head and shot himself.... I'm saddened by this, how can a man become so desperate after serving so many years in prison?

I look up Mauricio's former neighbor online. Sure enough, Marvin Amerson of Memphis, Tennessee, held up a bank just months after his release. The local news story features a cop speculating that getting out of prison must be frustrating: "Not being able to get a job or start over ... you know, forget his past, that's what he gets back into doing."[22] A message posted by Amerson's son on Instagram was more straightforward: "Daddy I've been without you for 21 years and when you finally get home it's only for four months. Now you are gone forever. RIP Pops."

So, the "session with shade" doesn't end as the Greyhound bus rolls out of the prison town, pointing toward "home." There's usually no dazzling morning, the sun predictably sliding through its journey across the curve of the sky. Usually, for former prisoners, when the sun comes, it's someone else's sun.

"Stuck on Stupid"

Mauricio, who has now served almost three decades in prison, confesses that when the same folks continually pop in and out of the doors, he sometimes gets angry—he feels they're not acknowledging that they play a role in whether or not they return. He reserves a special name for a few recidivists who he thinks *could* have made non-crime-related choices upon release, but didn't: Stuck on Stupid (SOS). ("SOS" rings doubly in my ears—in addition to bad decision-making, it suggests the desperation that characterizes the circumstances of so many returning prisoners.) At one point during our correspondence, three recently released young men reappear in his prison. Mauricio's so disappointed he can barely speak to them, he tells me; it kills him to see people "messing up" the chance he dearly wishes he'd had himself—the chance for a middle age spent outside the walls. Upon coming face to face with the young man he knows best, Mauricio says, "I just stared at him hard and said, 'You must really like it here.' Then I turned and walked away."

The concept of "stuck" brings to mind a poem written by incarcerated poet Etheridge Knight, in response to Gwendolyn Brooks's question, "When sun comes, how shall we greet him?" It is a meditation on the incomplete successes of the civil rights movement—a poem weighted with the continued oppression and incarceration of black people, despite the on-paper granting of many new "rights." It also offers a vivid, sobering commentary on the effects of imprisonment. Knight begins:

The sun came, Miss Brooks,—
After all the night years.
He came spitting fire from his lips.
And we flipped—We goofed the whole thing.
It looks like our ears were not equipped
For the fierce hammering.

And then later:

The Sun came, Miss Brooks.
And we goofed the whole thing.
I think.
(Though ain't no vision visited my cell.)

Release does not necessarily mean freedom, and rights do not necessarily mean reality, especially for formerly incarcerated people of color. "Stuck on Stupid"—"goofing the whole thing"—may illustrate the consequences of a system founded on disposability and isolation. When one's ears are accustomed to silence, a sound is jarring. And when one's mind and body are cordoned off from the rest of the universe, and are subsequently cast out, support-less, the effect can be paralyzing. This is not to say that formerly incarcerated people can't—or don't—make *choices.* But post-prison, the choices one can make are so limited by poverty, oppression, severed relationships, scant job and housing possibilities, and a felon label that it's often extremely difficult to choose well.

And so almost no one emerges from prison to the music of freedom bells, but instead to "fierce hammering"—the harsh sounds of a world to which they're ill-accustomed, a world that has forgotten them, a world that shuns them, a world in which it's all too easy to get "stuck."

"You'll Get Through It"

In mid-June, my parents and I drive four hours to central Illinois to visit Kayla at Logan Correctional Center. Unlike her previous prison, Kayla's current abode is a medium/maximum-security facility, and she has been assigned to a "maximum" unit. It's a strange placement. The offense for which she's incarcerated this time, we now know, is the theft of a bottle of perfume, intended to be a Christmas present. (She's stolen before, usually planning to sell the items for heroin money, but this time she got caught.) However, this spot is the location where almost all of Illinois' pregnant prisoners are placed. Kayla is now housed with women who are serving very long sentences, and seeing the years that stretch out before them seems to have a sobering effect. Kayla had a big group of friends—affectionately referred to as "my girls!"— her last time down, but she's not looking to re-create the scene. As we sit down at our table, after Kayla has hugged us so tightly that our ribs ache a bit afterward, she says, "I just want to keep my head down and do my time."

We move on to an extended debate about what to purchase from the vending machine, and settle on Fritos, strawberry milk, and an immense packaged cinnamon bun. I am dispatched, as Kayla is not allowed to get up. But I promptly fail my mission. Glum and distracted, I leave our prepaid vending machine card— no cash is allowed in the prison—in one of the machines after my first purchase. Only the strawberry milk is salvaged. I return to the machine after realizing my mistake and ask, "Has anyone seen my card? It had $20 on it."

"Ugh, *My*," Kayla groans, humiliated. "This is *prison!* You're not gonna see that card again."

Resigned, I hold the milk carton out to her. She shakes her head.

"I can't even think about it," she says, and it takes me a second to understand that she doesn't mean the milk. "It's just gonna be so hard this time."

You'll get through it, we say, though none of us can imagine carrying out a pregnancy while in prison, along with the agonizing anticipation of separation from her baby.

"I know," Kayla says. "But what am I going to do?"

"Just think about the day you get out," I say.

She pauses, and I realize again that we are talking about very different things.

"OK," she says. "But what am I going to do the day after that?"

Chapter 5

Disposable Babies

She's in the free world, so there are security considerations.
—Prison guard, explaining why Kayla can't call us from
the hospital after giving birth

It's late July and humidity drenches the sweat-scented air of the visiting room at Logan prison. Kayla is shifting back and forth in her stiff chair, tugging at her pink polo shirt, which is standard attire for incarcerated pregnant women. The pink identifies them as particularly vulnerable bodies, should "something happen." (The example Kayla gives is a physical fight: A person will get in more trouble, she says, if her adversary is pregnant.) She pushes impatiently at her belly, which is beginning to usurp the rest of her body. "I'm just moving Angelica around," she explains. "She's getting up in my rib cage." Kayla's a month and a half from her due date. We ask if her fellow prisoners avoid the topic of the pregnancy. Kayla shakes her head.

"People put their hands on my baby, and say, 'Aww, when is she due,' and I'm thinking, Who the hell did you murder?" she says, rolling her eyes. Logan houses all but three of the women convicted of homicide in Illinois. Kayla heaves her long hair into a pile atop her head, dark drizzles of makeup residue sliding out the corners of her eyes. "The next day, I find out. Oh great, you killed your kid! And your *dog*? Thanks for the good luck." She smiles. Kayla's sense of humor may be floundering a bit, given her current pool of material, but she's still got it.

Murder jokes notwithstanding, Kayla often reminds me not to make assumptions about people based on their conviction. She's friends with women convicted of murder—women who, in the midst of gang violence or domestic violence or any number of circumstances, made one horrible decision that condemned them for the rest of their lives. "Those crimes happened within a few minutes, usually," she says. "And then they're here forever."

The clock inches toward our visit's 7:30 departure time. We scoot closer, and Kayla grabs each of our hands to put on her belly. We feel the baby kicking. "Do you feel her now? *Now?*" she asks, and turns to Mom with a sudden, eager grin. "Are you excited to be a grandma?"

As we hurry back out to the car, I'm laughing and forgetting about the heat, bouncing a little as I make my way through the somber, emptying parking lot. The circumstances are wretched, but still—I'm going to be an aunt!

"I Want to Hold Her Forever"

At 4:47 a.m. on September 3, 2013, Mom wakes me up with news—"Kayla called she's on her way to the hospital she's really scared naturally whoa I can't believe this is happening!" No one really can, including Kayla. Her water hasn't broken, and she's not having contractions. Yet, at the convenience of the prison, her labor has been scheduled for today: It will be induced.

Mom and I commence waiting by our phones. No family can be present during labor and birth. Kayla's only company will be medical personnel and prison guards, who must watch her at all times. At some point after the birth, she'll get one phone call to let us know the baby has arrived. Once Angelica is born, Kayla will have twenty-four to thirty-six hours with her. Then the baby will be taken away, and Kayla will return to prison by herself.

I've never seen someone give birth in real life. My images of it, culled from movies, books, and friends, all feature groups of anxious, excited loved ones clustered inside and outside the birthing room, radiating warmth and comfort, preparing to ring in a time of communal celebration. I can't imagine anyone having to go through it alone. Kayla will not only be alone but also literally confined to her hospital bed: As soon as she's given birth, she'll be shackled to the bedposts.

Finally, at 1 p.m. on Wednesday, Mom calls the prison and pleads for news. She's transferred around and finally handed off to a counselor. He doesn't have much information, he says, and he shouldn't be telling her anything, but here's what he knows: "Ten fifty-two a.m., seven pounds, five ounces."

"EEEEE!" I dance and cry around the kitchen. "Ten fifty-two, seven pounds, five ounces! Ten fifty-two, seven pounds, five ounces!"

Then I stop. Is Kayla OK, health-wise? How did she handle almost twenty-six hours of labor? Did she get to breastfeed? When will they be separated? Aside from weighing seven pounds and five ounces, what's Angelica like? How is she dealing with methadone withdrawal? (Kayla has been kept on a steady dosage of methadone over the past few months in prison.) How is Kayla taking the anticipation of a different kind of withdrawal—withdrawal from her baby, whom she's only just met? Mom redials the counselor and asks him why Kayla can't yet call.

"She's in the free world right now, so there are security considerations," she's told. The warden has taken the day off and can't authorize the call, and the guards in the hospital room haven't allowed Kayla to pick up the phone.

The free world. This was the phrase used in the Cold War era to distinguish the US and friends from their communist foes. This was the phrase Neil Young used, ironically, to describe many Americans' poverty and despair, in "Keep on Rockin' in the Free World." The American president is the "leader of the free world." I think, *In what "world" do America's incarcerated live (that is, when they're not giving birth alone except for the company of prison guards)? Who's responsible for that un-free world, where mothers are torn from their babies every day?*

Finally, my mom gets the "one call" from Kayla. She puts her on speaker and calls me in. Kayla's breathing rapidly, and I can't tell whether she's laughing or crying as she gasps, "Oh my God, she is so beautiful. And I love her, I love her, I love her, and I just want to hold her forever."

Angelica is wailing full-blast when Kayla holds her face up to the receiver.

In the background, Kayla is sobbing, "My little baby, she doesn't even know what's coming," and her voice is heavy with the weight of the prison-bound pregnancy, the lonely labor, the painful birth, the love-at-first-sight, the shackling, the dreaded moment of separation, and the eighty-one days of waiting to come.

A few hours after our conversation, Kayla is handcuffed and led away from her baby and back to prison.

When my parents and I visit Angelica in the hospital, long after Kayla's gone, she's wide-eyed, squirming in her tiny bassinet. Taped to the wall of her crib is a three-page note filled with my sister's neat, decorative handwriting: a list of instructions. *She likes the top of her mouth tickled with the tip of the pacifier or your finger. It helps her feed. She loves to be held. She loves when you hold her hand.* And on, and on. And then: *I love you so so much, baby. I promise I'll be home soon.*

"Sentenced to Lose Each Other"

Kayla's story is not unique. Four to seven percent of women entering prison are pregnant, and most carry to term.[1] No statistics exist on the availability of abortion in prison. While in theory, incarcerated women have the same constitutional reproductive rights as others, many incarcerated women find that a request for an abortion is met with denial, delay, or dismissal.[2]

For the vast majority of prisoners who carry to term, the birth is a solitary and secretive affair, barred to family and loved ones. The following weeks, or months, or years are ravaged by one of the most excruciating breeds of isolation concocted by humanity: the separation of mothers from their babies. Even if a mother's sentence is short (on average, pregnant prisoners spend six to twelve months incarcerated after the birth[3]),infants may not remember their mothers upon release. Newly released moms often struggle to know their kids, as well. The two must reacquaint—like strangers—kicking off this most important relationship on a broken foot. For prisoners, who have already been severed from their communities, the mother–baby bond can forge a key path to societal reconnection, heightening their chances of avoiding reoffense and recidivism.[4] Conversely, severing the bond can feel like yet another way (and perhaps the most painful way) they're cut off from the "free world."

This isn't just true for babies born while their moms are incarcerated. It's true for prisoner moms across the board. (And there are a lot of them—nearly two-thirds of women in prison are mothers.[5]) In fact, studies show that mothers separated from their kids are more likely to be subsequently incarcerated. A 2004 study of mothers at New York City's jail showed that "family preservation efforts may function as a crime reduction strategy. Successful efforts to avert placement not only keep families together and children out of foster care, but can also help prevent the increase in maternal criminal activity that can take place following a child's removal."[6]

Instead, many mothers end up permanently losing custody of their kids: Due to long distances, visitation barriers, and extended periods of separation, lots of moms aren't able to meet court-mandated benchmarks required for reunification with their children upon release.[7] Even though Kayla will be released in just two and a half months, the Department of Child and Family Services pays her an unexpected visit in the days after the birth, intimating she may not be reunited with her child due to her current incarceration and prior drug use.

Scholar Beth Richie points to child protective services as yet another arm of the prison nation, using stringent regulations, surveillance, and policing to punish women—particularly black women, poor women, and single mothers—by taking away their kids.[8] Especially since the passage of the federal Adoption and Safe Families Act in 1997, incarcerated mothers have struggled to hang on to their children. The act's stringent reunification timeframes push foster care agencies to begin termination proceedings if a child has been in foster care for fifteen of the past twenty-two months. The majority of states usually do not include exceptions for moms in prison.[9] Plus, as legal scholar Dorothy Roberts notes, the restrictions on employment, housing, education, and public aid placed on mothers released from prison mean that, even after they've "reentered," formerly incarcerated moms are at a steep disadvantage when it comes to meeting the requirements of child protective services.[10] Bolstered by a distorted logic of "protecting" kids, the entwined forces of incarceration and foster care have bent toward the punishment of both mothers and children, with moms and kids of color receiving the brunt of "protective" attention.

Like Kayla's story, Angelica's circumstances—the separation that "she doesn't even know is coming"—are not unusual. Yet compared to many babies born to prisoners, Angelica is lucky. She has family on the outside who can care for her, though it won't be easy. My mother will be taking her in, with help from me and my dad, until Kayla's release. Many babies born in prison are shipped off to foster families and may never be able to visit their moms. More than half of the mothers in prison never see their kids while they're incarcerated.[11] Thus, prisoners' newborns are effectively sentenced along with their mothers.

Such sentencing may carry a premonition of further sentencing, of the sort that happens in a courtroom: Kids whose parents are incarcerated are more likely to engage in "criminal activity."[12] They're more prone to drug addiction, and they tend to lag behind on the education front. Many such behaviors are attributed to "attachment disorders"—a conditioned inability to connect. According to the American Psychological Society, babies who establish a strong bond with their mothers develop higher self-esteem and are better able to cultivate relationships later in life. For children born into the system, who don't develop the links that materialize in those earliest months, deep attachment issues can set in. Studies have shown that young kids with incarcerated mothers become more conflicted and detached, not only from their moms, but also from other caregivers.[13]

Compounding the situation, the vast majority of babies born to incarcerated moms can't breastfeed, denying both of them the possibility of one of the most intimate human bonds—and a source of health benefits that last years after nursing ends. Beyond nursing, it's been shown that babies whose moms are locked up have diminished chances of survival. According to Ernest Drucker's *A Plague of Prisons*, an examination of prison's effects through a public health lens, the impact of parental incarceration on infant mortality rates is undeniable: "Recent parental incarceration … independently affects infant mortality, elevating the risk of early infant death by 29.6 percent."[14] Given the demographics of who is in prison, infants of color are at an overwhelmingly greater risk than other groups.

As I watch Kayla and Angelica struggle with their separation, I think, *Wouldn't supporting mothers and babies in their lives together do a lot more to foster "public safety" than separating them?* What's the point of isolating these women, breaking their strongest ties to the outside world—their greatest motivators to "do better" upon release? Shouldn't we use the vast resources poured into their incarceration to bolster the difficult but toweringly important task of motherhood?

A week after Angelica's birth, my parents and I visit the hospital nursery, where the baby lies in her isolette, which is plastered with Kayla's notes. I see Kayla in Angelica's mouth, her eyes, the tensing of her forehead. She is, indeed, so beautiful—the softest, smallest, most earnest person I have ever seen. Someone places her in my lap, and she wriggles impatiently, her mouth wide open; she wants to nurse. She's out of luck on that front.

I stare down at the nineteen-inch human sprawled in my awkward arms. As she drifts off to sleep, I think, *I know what she's dreaming inside that delicate, perfect head.* It's no mystery. She wants her mom.

The Prison Nursery

In rare circumstances, babies born to prisoners aren't yanked from their mothers at birth. A very small number of those newborns simply travel back to prison with them. It's a controversial practice. On the one hand, it means imprisoning people at birth—people who've been convicted of no crime. This is not to say their mothers *should* be incarcerated, but that even under the current system's logic, the prospect of incarcerating babies is discomfiting. On the other hand, allowing children in prison means maintaining some vestige of the vital maternal attachment that's demolished for so many prisoner moms and their kids.

Until the 1950s, it was not uncommon for babies born in prison to stay with their mothers in prison-based nurseries, but the practice evaporated during the incarceration boom of the past forty years.* A few nurseries have recently reemerged in small-scale scenarios, like Illinois' much-hyped Moms and Babies program, which allows babies to remain with their mothers throughout infancy—but permits a grand total of eight babies at a time.[15]

Moms and Babies is located at Decatur prison, where Kayla spent her first state penitentiary bid. I remember well her condemnation of the program as she observed it firsthand, long before her own pregnancy. "It doesn't make sense that it has to be inside of a prison," she said. "They're only letting women into this program who have nonviolent offenses and good behavior, people they could let out if they wanted. So why can't they just let them *out*, instead of letting their babies come *in*?"

A debate currently rages among policymakers, experts, and intellectuals about whether the prison nursery is a cold sentence

---

* A notable exception is the nursery program at Bedford Hills prison in New York, which has existed continuously since 1901 and allows some babies to remain with their mothers until they're eighteen months old.

or the better of many evils—a practical mitigation of the effects of a destructive system that would otherwise simply break the mother–baby bond. Plus, mothers who participate in the nursery programs show lower recidivism rates.[16] However, if mothers' sentences continue past the age limit for babies in prison (the most lenient program allows them to stay no longer than thirty months), the bonds will still be torn.

Author Deborah Jiang-Stein, who was born in a federal prison in West Virginia, remained with her mother—in her cell—for the first year of her life. She visited the prison many years later, and she tells me, "The area felt familiar, even the smells and some of the buildings in the prison. It's emotional memory… I was keenly aware of it as I walked the prison compound."

I get in touch with Deborah in fall 2013. Kayla's in prison, Angelica is in the hospital, and Deborah is working on her memoir, *Prison Baby*, about her early upbringing in prison and subsequent separation from her mother. Her views on "prison babies" don't fit into a tidy box. Deborah's penitentiary year (her first twelve months on earth) allowed her to form a strong maternal bond—a bond that would be cut only when Deborah was removed from prison and placed in foster care, while her mother continued to do her time. "I was only removed because they didn't know what else to do with me," she says, pointing out that in the years before 1980—when many fewer people and many, *many* fewer women were incarcerated—were "uncharted years for how to handle pregnant inmates and babies born in prison."

She doesn't see her early months in prison as a clear-cut negative. "I believe my year of bonding with my birth mother set the stage for future stability," she says. "However, the separation from her and my placement in foster care also set the stage for trauma, self-doubt, and insecurity." Deborah's birth mother fought to keep her child, but, still incarcerated, lost the battle, and Deborah was adopted by her foster family. She and her birth mother never saw each other again, and years later Deborah discovered she'd died of cancer.

Experimenting with New Ways of Life

A movement has recently emerged that calls for programs that allow new mothers to live outside prison in restricted community housing with their children. Deborah points to the benefits of this approach: "If it allows for visiting and nurturing contact, that can only help a baby." Advocates note that community-based programs have all the benefits of a prison nursery without the downsides and are both more humane and more effective. According to the Women's Prison Association,[17] infants and moms clearly fare better when they're not separated, and community-based residential parenting programs have been shown to "protect public safety and reduce recidivism at a fraction of the human and economic costs of prison."

However, these programs can blur into the realm of imprisonment, operating out of a framework of punishment and confinement—a manifestation of the prison nation. In a University of Illinois study of "The House," a community-based "correctional alternative" for new mothers, "an underlying tension existed between social services and corrections objectives. Despite a services orientation, many residents and staff perceived the House environment as punitive." Recidivism was low among those who completed the program, but a third of the participants didn't complete it—and most of those women were reincarcerated. The study also raised an uncomfortable issue: If mothers are externally confined with their babies—sometimes with "unnecessary restrictions on contact with other family members"—their relationships with their *other* kids, if they have them, may well suffer.[18]

The most successful programs seem to function within a wholly different framework: one of support and accountability, connections instead of "corrections." An encouraging example can be found in A New Way of Life (ANWOL), a chain of homes for recently incarcerated women in Los Angeles. The centers were founded by Susan Burton, a formerly incarcerated mother whose five-year-old son was killed by a speeding police car. Susan supports mothers in meeting the state's reunification requirements so they won't lose their kids to child protective services.[19]

Along with providing women and their kids with their basic needs, ANWOL offers job training and assistance with case management—as well as opportunities to get involved with advocacy for a better system. ANWOL hosts the LEAD (Leadership, Education, Action, Dialogue) Project, a workshop that engages with the political and social systems that perpetuate the prison nation, emphasizing the targeting of black and brown people and the ways in which frameworks of isolation instill themselves in every corner of society.[20] Women have the opportunity to get involved with All of Us or None, a movement of formerly incarcerated people working to restore the rights of people with past convictions, so mothers can not only work toward their own reunification with their kids, but work to change the system for future women in their shoes.[21]

"And Then What?"

In the weeks after Angelica is born, whenever I have to tell someone about Kayla's continued incarceration, I get a response like, "But what's the *point*?" Or, "How is Kayla being in prison helping anyone?" I am thinking but not saying, "How is *anyone* being in prison helping anyone?"

There are a couple of reasons why my friends and family members see this question so clearly when it comes to Kayla: 1) They know her, or at least they know me, and they don't see me as someone whose family member "should" be in prison, given my privileged place in society; 2) She has been separated from her baby, an occurrence that feels viscerally wrong. However, the "what's the point?" response also prompts a vital question that, I think, should play a central role in any system of justice. That question is, "And then what?"

In a 2012 speech, Glenn E. Martin, founder of the organization JustLeadershipUSA, which aims to cut the prison population in half by 2030, suggests: "At sentencing, we must ask our judges, 'And then what?' When the head of our police department decides that aggressive policing is the way to public safety, we must ask, 'And then what?' When our governors tinker around the edges by right-sizing prisons instead of downsizing the system, we must ask, 'And then what?'" In other words, if the goal of "justice" is not simply revenge, we must have a route to amelioration in mind, every step of the way.[22]

Kayla stays in prison, mired in despair and futile anxiety, while her baby languishes at the hospital and then at "home" without her—and then what?

Deborah Jiang-Stein spends a year in prison as an infant, able to bond with her mother for twelve months behind bars—and then what?

Sable Kolstee is torn from her kids and prohibited by parole rules from seeing them, even upon release, knowing they're out there but not in her arms—and then what?

Joe Jackson spends the rest of his life in prison for a drug offense while his family struggles financially and emotionally without him—and then what?

Marcos Gray serves out juvenile life without parole, held prisoner to racism and poverty—and then what?

Has society gotten better because of these incarcerations? Have these prisoners "changed their ways"? Has prison "reformed" them, nineteenth-century-style? Have separation and disconnection worked their magic?

The topic of rehabilitation arises during a prison visit the week after Kayla has given birth. Kayla is morose, both physically sick and heartbroken, and every question we ask falls to the ground with a barely audible "yes" or "no."

"I'm taking a parenting class," she finally offers. "Yesterday we had a guest."

"Who?" I ask.

"Well," she says, "it was this lady who was locked up for like fifteen years. When she went in, her kids got taken away and went into foster care, and they stopped seeing her, talking to her, everything. Then finally she got out, and they didn't even *want* to see her."

"That's terrible!"

"*Eventually* her kids did start talking to her again, once they were adults," Kayla assures us. "And now they're pretty close. They can call each other up just to say hi, and everything.... But yeah—there's a lot of women in the class who've been in here forever, and they think their kids don't love them, and who knows, maybe they don't. So I guess the lesson is just, even if you've been gone a long time, you still might be able to get to know your kids."

And that is a parenting class, prison-style.

Angela Davis points to the irony of such classes: "In the jails and prisons where they are incarcerated, [women prisoners] are presumably being taught to be good mothers, even as they are powerless to prevent the state from seizing their own children."[23]

Deepening the irony, that "seizing" is more likely to happen if women admit to drug problems, seeking rehabilitation: "Their admissions are used as evidence of their incapacity to be good mothers."

Indeed, as the weeks tick down to Kayla's release from prison, the Department of Child and Family Services will pay her a visit. Because she has admitted to a drug addiction, she'll be told, she might be denied custody of her child, even after release.

On the afternoon of the parenting class conversation, as we're driving out of the parking lot, Mom provides a word of commentary: "Probably, a better parenting lesson would involve letting her actually spend time with her child."

And then we head off to the hospital to see Angelica, who's tucked into her nursery crib, alone.

And then what?

Part Two

Coming Together

Chapter 6

The Case for a Pen Pal

Only connect.
—*E. M. Forster*, Howard's End

Kayla's pregnancy and postbirth incarceration in 2013 breaks me of my nostalgic fondness for letters. The urgency of the situation—the baby—strains the space between us, and at this overcrowded prison letters take three weeks to be processed upon arrival. I am dropping envelopes in the mail slot with a kind of reckless uncertainty, knowing that many of my messages will fall useless into Kayla's lap, bearing outdated questions or now-irrelevant tips. But as our correspondence continues, I begin to think: The reason I once loved writing to Kayla was because it offered a chance for deep, sustained communication—a communication that doesn't usually happen between people who are, in so many ways, hundreds of miles apart.

I've corresponded with a couple of dozen prison pen pals over the past eight years. The "use" of pen-palship has made itself visible in small and large ways over the course of these loosely threaded friendships. Sometimes, a piercing phrase will spring up out of the envelope—a truth that will never leave my mind. At other times, a prisoner will contribute a vital bit of information that proves unavailable anywhere else. Often, though, the "use" of pen-palship is not in the particulars of what is being communicated, but in the act of communicating.

Prison is built on a logic of isolation and disconnection. Letters between pen pals are almost always exchanged for the opposite purpose and with the opposite effect: connection.

As summer dawns, I think a lot about how the act of penpalling is significant, not just for my relationship with my sister, but in the way it mirrors the mindset shift that will be necessary to rethink how our society "does justice" on a much larger scale. My conversations, correspondences, and relationships with prison-torn families have taught me that separation breeds more separation, that the coldness and isolation of prison breed the coldness and isolation of violence. And I think about how the one-on-one relationship, in which the prisoner emerges as a person (with thoughts, a personality, a history, hopes, dreams, nightmares), might serve as a model for the beginnings of a person-based, connection-based justice system.

The Person Steven Woods

In early 2006, I began working on a piece on prison-based activism for the music and politics magazine *Punk Planet*. I wanted to write about action happening on the inside, action that might not be getting any attention beyond the walls, and I began writing to people in prison to find out what they were thinking. I soon developed an ongoing correspondence with my first prison pen pal, Steven Michael Woods, who was on death row in Texas. Steven was leading a hunger strike to advocate for more humane—or, at least, marginally tolerable—conditions. Addressing the envelope

("Polunsky Unit," death row) scared me. My image of Steven was murky and amorphous, a silent symbol of the media label routinely slapped on death row prisoners: "worst of the worst." However, the day I received my first letter from this man, I came to the jarring, thudding realization that he was human. Not Inmate No. 1267, but the person, Steven Woods.

Steven was twenty-six, two years older than me. (He was arrested at twenty-one.) He worshipped '90s underground rock and had played bass and guitar for "beer party punk bands" in past days. His politics were passionate—and, incredibly, more hopeful than mine: He wrote of his belief in the power of nonviolent resistance to "help our fellows rise above their chains," even in the direst of circumstances. To top it off, he'd been an avid *Punk Planet* reader before he was locked up—he could name cover stories from 2001. He claimed he was innocent: His co-defendant, whose fingerprints were found on the weapons, had confessed to being the sole shooter in the murder. No physical evidence against Steven was ever discovered, although he did acknowledge being at the scene of the crime. (I neither questioned nor affirmed Steven's innocence throughout our correspondence, but I did go online and read, over and over, flooded with grief, anger, and confusion, the gory details of the murder he was said to have committed.) Now, he woke each morning sweating uncontrollably, hit with the stark inevitability of his impending death.

In his first letter to me, Steven shared that he was working on a zine—a handwritten, self-produced magazine filled with rants and comics—entitled "The Continuing Struggle of a Nail in My Coffin." The point? "To educate and entertain!" Steven wrote me. "Sitting idle while the world wallows in ignorance and apathy just isn't for me."

In my letters to Steven, I didn't talk much about my own life (though I answered his questions about the music scene here in Chicago, where he'd once lived). It felt absurd to blather on about my bland day job, lunchtime trips to Noodles and Company, and watching television marathons on DVD. So I asked what life was like in Polunsky, what protest actions he had planned for the future, and whether he had any appeals left to fight his sentence. "One more," he wrote.

My string of questions began wearing itself ragged. I was repeating myself, struggling to avoid the one topic that burned at the forefront of my mind and the tip of my pen. Our letters grew further apart. I tried to send him copies of *Punk Planet*; they didn't get through inspection. We "chatted" about protest behind bars. He wrote, "The biggest part of being an activist is reaching out and instilling the spirit of revolution and resistance in our fellows, to break the herd mentality … you place us into a situation where all the fuel is already there, and all it needs is a spark." I wrote, "I am so impressed with all you are doing!" I thought: "What good will any of it do? You're dying." We traversed light, safe, death-free discussion terrain: Chicago bookstores, my work at *Punk Planet*, the merits of Mountain Dew (which he loved and I hated). He wrote about the time of enlightenment that would come "after we win better conditions back here."

I avoided the mailbox, falling toward a selfish, gutless conclusion: I didn't want to watch Steven die. I stopped writing first.

For four years, I quit thinking about Steven, or tried. But in the summer of 2012, as I began this book, I combed through my letters from pen pal interviews past. There was Steven. And so I took a deep breath and googled "Steven Woods" and "Texas death row." The Internet delivered the news: My friend had been executed in 2011. His last meal had included French toast, bacon-topped pizza, chicken-fried steak, and, of course, Mountain Dew, though he hadn't eaten a bite. His last words: "Warden, if you're going to murder someone, go ahead and pull that trigger.... I love you Mom.... Goodbye, everyone. I love you."

Meeting the "Monster"

The poet Richard Shelton spent several decades leading writing workshops in Arizona prisons. His inspiration for the classes was an extended correspondence with a death row prisoner convicted of three murders. Shelton writes in his book *Crossing the Yard* of the first letter he received from Charles Schmid, who sought his advice about writing poetry. "Here was my chance, I thought, to read the poetry of a monster," recalls Shelton, "an exotic subspecies of human I had never encountered."[1]

But Shelton saw promise in Schmid's work, and they mailed poetry back and forth, sifting emotions and motivations and tangled histories as they sifted words. "I was beginning to realize, dimly, that I was dealing with a human being and that I could no longer think of my involvement as casual, as a form of literary slumming," Shelton writes.[2] Eventually he visited Schmid and began to extend his services and his friendship to other men in the maximum-security prison where Schmid was incarcerated.

Shelton's relationship with the "monster" yielded transformations in ways beyond the poetic. After four years of writing together, Schmid told Shelton, "I'm not the same person.... I'm only now beginning to realize, to understand, what I've done. Something's happened to me. Something wonderful and frightening. I can't explain it, but I feel like somebody else. And you are what made it happen."[3] Thirty years after he met Schmid, Shelton feels like somebody else, too—his prison workshops and friendships have "enriched and enlarged my life. It has led me through

bloody tragedies and terrible disappointments to a better understanding of what it means to be human and even, sometimes, to
triumph."[4]

It wasn't all fuzzy wuzzy, Shelton assures us: He wrestled with
the fact that many of his new buddies had committed acts of
extreme violence—acts that had deeply harmed people (real humans, too!) and families—and that these actions could not simply
be ignored. So although his link to the prison revolved around
poetry, and his role was that of an educator, Shelton nevertheless
became heavily immersed in his students' struggles, and troubled
by some of their crimes.

He writes of a note he sent prisoner Jimmy Baca, after receiving an ongoing litany of rants from Baca about his treatment in
prison. Shelton, fed up, wrote: "I don't see how anybody as smart
as you could be so stupid as to do something that would get you
sent to prison, where you knew you would be completely under
the control of those less intelligent than you are."[5] Though Shelton worried about how this would be received, the starkness of
those words on paper struck Baca hard, in the best way. He kept
the letter in his wallet for years and years thereafter, a reminder
that the system wasn't a one-way game: His actions played a part
in his predicament. (As Mauricio Rueben would say, he was a bit
"Stuck on Stupid.") Baca went on to become an award-winning
poet in his own right, and to be released from prison.

Shelton knows that his mentorship of Baca, Schmid, and others profoundly impacted their lives—but he also acknowledges
that poetry and friendship aren't "solutions" to incarceration. A
back-cover endorsement calls the poet's memoir "a moving plea
for the arts in prison." But Crossing the Yard actually calls for a
much more radical and real transformation: abolition of the prison system. Shelton did not start out as an activist; he was a poet

and teacher offering his services. His firsthand experience of getting to know prisoners as people awakened for him the power of those bonds to change worlds. It has transformed Shelton just as it transformed his pen pals, students, friends. And, he writes, it has caused him—rather, it has *forced* him—to imagine his way beyond a system that isolates people in a manner that, ordinarily, permits folks in Shelton's position to simply forget about them, unless they should chance to receive a letter from a "monster."

Their "Side of the Story"

In early 2013, Beth Derenne from the Women's Prison Book Project (WPBP) sends me a packet of thank-you letters from women who've participated in her book exchange. I flip through the pages, pausing on a letter from Sable Sade Kolstee, who describes herself as a book lover with a "thirsty brain." I drop her a note to see if she'll answer some questions for my book on prison and disconnection. She responds promptly in round, clear print: "I am 26 years old and a mother to 3 beautiful children. When you talk about disconnected—I was shut off from my children from April 4, 2010 until just this month, March 2013. My crime put restrictions on my contact with minors."

Sable writes achingly of how she's been severed from her three young kids, all under the age of eight. Over the course of her incarceration, Sable has missed a long list of early milestones: "first steps, concerts, growth, birthdays, holidays, and many more." Letters, calls *and* visits from her children have been banned until recently, she writes: "My greatest challenge was fighting for the children. So many times counselors would say 'I understand.' I would look at them and tell them not to lie to me because none of you have ever gone 1 year, 18 months, 2 years without your children."

The battle for her children won't end upon release, Sable says. The terms of her parole will also mandate a separation from her children. And, she writes, her "separation" extends beyond contact with her kids, and even beyond the limits of the law. She's worried about how people will perceive her. "It's not that I think I won't be able to make a positive contribution to society when I get out," she writes, "but the stigma I will live with for the next 22 years will possibly make me shy or frightened of judgment. Although I want to help others and show my children that a mistake does not define you."

At this point, I'm absorbed and pained; I feel for my new pen pal. And I'm rooting for her! But the gigantic thought bubble hanging over my brain is shouting, *"What was the mistake?"* What act would bar her from receiving visits from her kids—or leave her with a twenty-two-year postrelease "stigma"?

I google her, of course. One cruel irony prisoners face is that while they're behind bars, unable to speak for themselves, the Internet offers up a host of third-party information about them: mugshots, court documents, personal data (age, height, weight, tattoo verbiage), past records, and often-sensational press coverage of their convictions. A couple of newspaper snippets disclose that at twenty-three she was convicted of "statutory assault"—having a "sexual relationship" with a "known minor male" over the course of a couple of months, as evidenced by text messages exchanged between the two. I write Sable for her perspective on what happened.

Asking prisoners for their "side of the story" can be an awkward affair, something it doesn't even make sense to do unless the incarcerated person initiates the conversation; after all, the *story* is just one of each prisoner's stories—the act for which they're incarcerated doesn't define them—and the last thing a pen pal should be doing is implying that. Perhaps I shouldn't have broached the topic in the first place. But Sable's very straightforward: She "did it," she says. In her early twenties, she was attending college and caring for her three young children (including a newborn). The kids' father, Derrick, was in prison, and Sable, overwhelmed (she says she'd been "codependent" on Derrick), began to drink, use drugs heavily, and "sleep around with whoever." From there, she says, her judgment slid downhill. She began dating a guy who, a month and a half in, told her he was fifteen. They fought, he left—but he continued coming around at night for a couple of weeks, and Sable, drunk and lonely, suppressed her major qualms. "I thought, hell I did this at that age," she writes. The relationship soon ended, but Sable subsequently discussed it with a friend—who turned her in to the cops. She was charged with five counts of statutory sexual assault.

In the grand hierarchy of public perceptions of crime, ranging from I-don't-know-why-this-person-is-in-prison to this-person-is-despicable-scum, people incarcerated for sex offenses are categorically deposited into the "scum" pile. I'd never corresponded with someone in this position before, except for brief interview-style exchanges for articles. Honestly, if I hadn't impulsively written Sable based on her WPBP letter, I probably would've looked up her conviction and, glimpsing "sexual assault," ruled her out.

But I didn't, and now we were friends, and—though I didn't and still don't pretend to fully comprehend the ins and outs of her case—when she wrote of her hunch that if she'd had money for a decent lawyer, she'd "never have seen a day in prison," I thought, "She's probably right." I google "age of consent." In Spain, it's thirteen. In Austria and Bulgaria, it's fourteen. In Turkey, it's eighteen. In Costa Rica, it's fifteen. And in Pennsylvania, where Sable was convicted, it is sixteen; the boy with whom she had sex was fifteen years old. I wonder: What defines a sex crime, what makes someone a sex "criminal," and why am I so hesitant about writing to someone who's been branded with that label? I've had pen pals who have pled guilty to murder. Why am I even more insecure about corresponding with a woman who admits to a statutory sex offense? How do our definitions of "human" match up with our categories of "crime"? Questioning the labeling of a "sex criminal" is not to diminish the tragedy and trauma of rape, or the pain of survivors, who are often underrecognized, ignored, or even punished in our culture. Rather, it's about questioning the logic of a system in which a person becomes defined by one of their acts—defined *as* that act instead of as a person. The questions knock at my brain. Sable and I continue to write.

For most of her prison sentence, Sable was barred from seeing or speaking with her children, but just before she's released she is granted one visit. When the day comes, her oldest kid remembers her right away, and she's "loving, excited and quite the chatterbox," Sable writes me. Her three-year-old boy is understandably shy; for most of his life, his mother has been invisible. Meanwhile, her middle child stays quiet, rarely smiles, and looks down a lot. Eventually, though, she gazes up at Sable and asks whether she can "live with [her] forever."

The answer is no. After Sable is released, she'll still be held tightly in the prison nation's grip. She will spend three years on parole, held to an 8 p.m. curfew each night. She writes that she can't have a driver's license, and must avoid the Internet, cell phones, "excessive amounts of candy," and "contact with minors"—including her own children. Her conflicted feelings squeeze through the lines of her letters—her desperation for freedom, her fear of long-term separation from her kids, her longing for fresh air, her anxieties around the millions of unknown people who will share that fresh air with her. But a few days before departure, she says she's ready. She writes to me: "I have a long list of things I have to do. The first thing I'm doing is eating a pizza. After that, my steps towards my new life can begin."

I wasn't expecting an update on that "new life," let alone the pizza. But a month later, I'm delighted to find a letter from Sable in my box, this one sent from her grandmother's house in New York. "I did have pizza my first day out—it was SO good," she writes. She's also enjoying the series of small decisions that comprise her days on the outside: picking out her clothes, cooking a meal, choosing to go for a barefoot walk along the nearby river … as long as she's sure—as sure as one can be—that she will not come across a minor. Indeed, there are many choices she can't make. She can't find a job, so is tethered to her "Gram" (who loves her but is prone to getting "worked up into a tizzy"). She still can't see her kids. And her face is plastered on a sex offender registry for the next twenty-two years. Months later, I receive a short note from Sable: "Being on parole is the hardest thing ever." I wrack my brain for encouraging things to say—but "Hey, you're getting out soon!" doesn't work anymore. I end up simply writing, "I'm so sorry."

Feel Uncomfortable!

For deeper insight into the emotional and political roles of the pen pal, I turn to Rev. Jason Lydon of Boston. If there's such thing as a prison pen-pal guru, it's Jason. His group Black and Pink focuses on helping prisoners connect directly with pen pals on the outside, building both friendships and action-based relationships that link people through the bars. Jason has been incarcerated himself, and many of his own pen pals are people he left behind in prison. He sees pen-palship as a way to "dispel myths about who's incarcerated … it's necessary for people to recognize that it's human beings who are being locked up, denied access to health care, assaulted."

I'm struck by the way he talks about the pen-pal process as active and transformative: It's not just about making friends. And, he tells me, if you're fully engaged in the process, it's probably not always going to be easy. You can't keep your pen pal in a box. (That's not what you're there for—they're in a box already!)

"We need to challenge ourselves on why we're creating certain boundaries," Jason says, when I ask about navigating the sometimes-weird personal terrain of pen-palship. "Are we setting those boundaries to make ourselves feel *comfortable*, or to make ourselves feel safe? Allowing ourselves to feel uncomfortable can help us grow, and to build authentic relationships and understandings. Being uncomfortable at times is OK, as long as we're still safe."

Once, I wrote a column for *Truthout* urging readers to link up with pen pals in prison. I was overjoyed to receive a number of responses from eager people seeking prisoners to write. But within two months, a couple of readers contacted me to say they'd cut off their newfound pen-palships. One prisoner pen pal had begun a series of overtly romantic overtures, ignoring the outside pen pal's cues. Another had persisted in making openly misogynist remarks, even after his outside pen pal told him it upset her. It's inevitable that, sometimes, you won't get along with your pen pal. It's another "side effect" of the fact that they're human.

I think of my own abandoned pen pals. One expressed such blatant homophobia in a letter that I couldn't bring myself to respond. I didn't want to start a conflict but didn't want to implicitly agree—so I stuffed his letter in a drawer. The other, of course, was Steven Woods; I had quit writing simply because I didn't want to face the emotional avalanche of his impending execution, and I will always regret it.

According to Jason, the emotional avalanches are part of the point. In fact, he notes, the eruption of issues like misogyny, racism, homophobia, and transphobia may be a touchstone for important conversations, especially since, when we write to people in prison, we're in a separate physical space. The medium of letters lends time to process words and contemplate responses. Jason tells me, "My hope is that people would be willing to extend a little more patience toward people on the inside than they would to folks on the outside, because of the amount of safety that we experience as folks who aren't incarcerated." He points to situations, for example, in which white prisoners have made racist statements in letters; pen pals have sometimes challenged those statements and engaged in productive dialogues (though Jason emphasizes that people of color shouldn't feel any obligation to "be patient" in such situations, and if safety feels threatened, it is always OK to walk away). And it's a two-way street: Your pen pal may call you out on assumptions and biases you never realized you had.

As a former prisoner, Jason knows the value of outside ties firsthand, especially for particularly marginalized groups of prisoners, who are regularly exposed to excruciating treatment. When he was locked up in a segregated unit for queer, trans, and gender-nonconforming prisoners and repeatedly subjected to cruel treatment and sexual violence at the hands of guards, he vowed to remain in touch with his fellow prisoners upon release. "For those of us who have been incarcerated," he says, the pen pal process serves as "a reminder to not forget folks who are left behind, that we have a responsibility to maintain relationships and compassion with those folks, to join in the healing process with them."

Concretely, he says, aside from expanding our boundaries and awareness and engaging in dialogue, there are a few very immediate purposes for a pen pal. Receiving letters during mail call can serve as a function that resembles the other definition of "mail": a protective shield against potential violence. As noted earlier, it alerts guards that you've got contacts and advocates on the outside, so you're less likely to be mistreated. Such "mail" is also useful when it comes to prisoners potentially harming themselves. Self-injurious behavior is common, and "having a reminder that you're cared for and not forgotten—and part of a larger thing—can help you deal with the mental and emotional struggle that is the reality of being locked up."

"We Cannot Be Passive Recipients"

In the book *Howard's End*, E. M. Forster wrote his instructions on the best way to live in two short words: "Only connect." (E. M. Forster, incidentally, also announced on the BBC, in a fiery 1934 critique of the mechanization and industrialization of society, "Prison is no good."[6])

When we reach out to a prisoner to "only connect," we will always—to some extent—fail, because the barriers are so vast and so entrenched. But there are few cases in which a personal act that takes so little time can make such a great difference. *I encourage anyone with the time, capacity, and emotional energy for it to reach out.* In the appendix of this book there is a list of resources to help you become a pen pal. If you're reading this book (and I know you are—or at least you're reading this page), flip on back.

Before diving in, pen pals should check in with themselves, issuing a stern reminder that the act of writing a prisoner is not an act of *charity*. It's about growing a unique breed of friendship. In fact, it's one of the few contexts where you're able to throw out a line to a stranger and say, "Will you be my friend?" It is an act that is not driving toward any clear, ostensible goal. Rather, it's the goal-less endeavor of "getting to know" another person, which, for whatever reason, can be one of the most fulfilling, interesting, and transformative things to do in life. It's also a primary building block for any greater political possibility that relies on connection between human beings—which, it seems, applies to every viable political possibility under the sun.

As the Illinois-based pen-pal collective Write to Win puts it: "We see individual correspondence with people on the inside as one piece of the larger struggle to abolish the prison-industrial complex and to create safe, sustainable, and equitable communities. To this end, we see our work as a way to undermine the isolation, dehumanization, and destruction of the PIC by building grassroots networks of support and solidarity between folks on the inside and folks on the outside."[7] In other words, how can policy change—or, for that matter, deep systemic change—evolve, if outside activists and theorists and advocates aren't talking *to* the people they're talking about?

Lacino Hamilton, my pen pal in Michigan, emphasizes that prisoners need to vocalize their experiences, and an outside audience is key. "We cannot be passive recipients of the efforts of others," he writes. "We have to be part of the work being done."

What efforts—and what work? Well. The pen-pal journey is certainly not the endgame; it's the *beginning* game. Perhaps, then, "*Only* connect" is not a perfect motto. Lacino's words highlight the potential of prisoners' connections with outside allies to build creative new models, initiatives, movements—maybe even revolutions!—that cultivate a more just world.

Chapter 7

Working from the Inside Out: Decarcerate!

This could be your brother, your son, or your father. This is
what's in our future. We have to stop it.
—Reginald Akkeem Berry, on the need to
oppose supermax prisons

In 2006, a letter was slipped in through the door slat in Johnnie
Walton's cell. Johnnie was living—twenty-three hours a day—in
a seventy-square-foot cell furnished with a concrete bed, a solid steel door, and a window through which little light traveled.
Through the slat in the door, three times a day, Johnnie's meals
appeared. For one hour each day, Johnnie was permitted solitary
"recreation" in a small pen just outside his cell.

The same routine went for the roughly 250 other prisoners
in Tamms, the supermax prison that had opened in Southern
Illinois in 1998. Practices at Tamms were similar to those in
other supermax prisons and "Secure Housing Units" (such as
the one Abraham Macías occupies at Pelican Bay) around the
country: The prison, with no yard, no chapel, no dining hall,
no library, and no phone calls (unless a close relative was dying), was designed to extinguish the outside world for the men
trapped within.

By the time the letter came, Johnnie had already been living in isolation for more than two years. He tore open the envelope and stared. Tucked inside was a poem. An accompanying letter explained that the sender was a member of the "Tamms Poetry Committee," a group that had come together to provide some contact for these men deprived of almost every type of human connection.

Johnnie was touched but bewildered, he tells me over the phone, almost eight years later. "I got that letter, and I thought, 'A poetry committee? Men are mutilating themselves, slitting their wrists here.... What do we need with a poetry committee?'"

Johnnie wrote back with a thank-you note—but the note went further: He asked for help, for advocacy. So did several of the other men who received poems that year. Artist and activist Laurie Jo Reynolds, who was part of the group that initiated the poetry committee and later led the effort to fight for the rights of Tamms prisoners, told me, "Not to insult us, but at the beginning, it was sort of a social club. It was the men who wrote to us and told us, 'It's time to do more. You have to tell people what's happening to us in here.'"

Doing more meant mounting a broad-based organizing effort to confront the conditions at—and, later, the existence of—Tamms. (They dubbed the campaign "Tamms Year Ten," referencing the fact that, though there was supposed to be a one-year limit on prisoners' stay at the supermax, many had remained there the entire ten years of its existence.) It meant meeting with legislators at every chance possible and graphically describing the conditions in the prison, guided by the words of the men inside. It meant vigils, press conferences, lobbying days at the capitol, and a community picnic complete with a parsley-eating contest. Tamms Year Ten partnered with dozens of other organizations and sympathetic legislators, mobilizing for a reform bill limiting terms at Tamms and requiring prisoners to be told why they were transferred to the supermax. At the forefront of the struggle were family members of men hidden away in the prison. As several Tamms prisoners were released (by way of parole, appeal victories, or the end of their sentences), they became leaders in the campaign.

In fact, the day that Johnnie got out, he swallowed his postrelease anxieties and spoke of his years in Tamms to a large crowd at a fundraiser in a Chicago nightclub. "It was scary," he says. "There was lots of noise ... but I had to start right away, speaking for the people who didn't have a voice. I had to speak about the torture of Tamms."

Reginald Akkeem Berry, another former Tamms prisoner, says that advocating for the men he'd left behind in the supermax was tough at first, partly because they were essentially invisible, knocked off the map at the bottom of Illinois without so much as a phone call home. "Most people didn't know the town of Tamms, Illinois, even existed," Akkeem says. So when he spoke about the prison, he invoked people on the outside instead. He spoke of family and the ways that solitary confinement harms poor black and brown communities—especially at a time when the Illinois prison population was still rising and supermaxes were multiplying across the country. "Every time I went to a community meeting, I said, these people in Tamms—this could be your brother, your son, or your father. This is what's in our future. We have to stop it."

Akkeem was the first released man to be interviewed about Tamms, he says, for a 2008 *Chicago Reader* feature titled "Hell in a Cell." At that point, "solitary confinement" was a phrase most folks on the outside hadn't often heard. Media attention intensified. In 2009, the work of Tamms Year Ten caught the attention of Amnesty International, which condemned the prison as "incompatible with the USA's obligations to provide humane treatment for all prisoners."[1]

The folks of Tamms Year Ten spoke before legislative budget hearings. In addition to denouncing the human destruction occurring behind Tamms' walls, they pointed to the prison's staggering price tag: holding one prisoner at Tamms cost $92,000 per year.[2] Momentum against Tamms caught fire—and increasingly, caught the eye of Illinois Governor Pat Quinn. Meanwhile, the prison guards unions and the town of Tamms fought hard to keep the prison, and the struggle unfolded in the media and in the streets, with prisoners' families lobbying at the state capital and leading marches in Chicago.

In 2012, despite the many legislators vying for Tamms to stay open, the governor performed a rare line-item veto and simply budgeted Tamms out of existence. Despite challenges by the legislature, the Illinois Supreme Court decided to permit this move, and in January 2013 the prison was shuttered. Tamms Year Ten had triumphed.

There's more: When Quinn performed his act of line-item rebellion, he also ordered the closing of three other Illinois prisons, citing cost savings. Those included two youth prisons whose elimination had been advocated by Project NIA and other groups, through efforts like a hunger strike, legislative advocacy, and community organizing.[3] Also included was Dwight, a maximum-security women's prison. The Illinois prison system seemed to be shrinking.

Decarcerate!

Shrinking: In a country where more than 7 million people are bound up in the "correctional" system, this is how many people working against incarceration frame their goal. You can't pop this balloon with just one pin. Not everyone working to close Tamms was interested in abolishing all prisons, but many were. They were simply starting with one.

Historian and activist Dan Berger points to the importance of such concrete change-making—closing buildings, reducing prison populations, slashing budgets, dismantling policies that confine people even after release—to the overall goal of freeing ourselves from the prison nation. He defines this movement as *decarceration*: "reform in pursuit of abolition."[4]

The word "incarcerate" stems from the same root as the word "cancel": Both mean to cross something, or someone, out (whether with bars, or lines, or actions). Decarceration, then, is also a movement toward *un*-canceling people—not just by fighting for their release, but by recognizing and supporting their humanity.

The strategy that drove the Tamms Year Ten campaign was about making visible the lives of people who'd been "canceled" in the most extreme way. And Tamms was not the only place in which people in solitary confinement were finding ways to come together and speak out. In fall 2012, more than a year after they'd waged two three-week hunger strikes, prisoners in California's Pelican Bay SHU announced a historic Agreement to End Hostilities, which was then signed and publicized by thousands of people inside and outside of prison, building a coalition across the state. It read, in part:

> Beginning on October 10, 2012, all hostilities between our racial groups ... in SHU, Ad-Seg, General Population, and County Jails, will officially cease. This means that from this date on, all racial group hostilities need to be at an end ... and if personal issues arise between individuals, people need to

do all they can to exhaust all diplomatic means to settle such disputes; do not allow personal, individual issues to escalate into racial group issues.... Collectively, we are an empowered, mighty force, that can positively change this entire corrupt system..., and thereby, the public as a whole.

Prisoners emphasized that their actions extended beyond a pursuit of reforms. They were challenging the prison nation's assumption of—and instigation of—ongoing "racial warfare" behind bars, which is used to justify solitary confinement and other restrictive policies meant to isolate prisoners from each other.

In June 2013, when prisoners in the Pelican Bay SHU waged a nonviolent hunger strike to demand better conditions and more opportunities to connect with people on the outside, building networks that fostered both action and visibility were key. Tens of thousands of California prisoners fasted in solidarity. An outside movement led by family members of the strikers rose up across the state and across the country to support the prisoners with letters, phone calls to the Department of Corrections, and rallies. The strike garnered unprecedented media attention, appearing in many major newspapers and on radio and television stations.

Isaac Ontiveros of the prison abolitionist organization Critical Resistance tells me about the group's participation in the strike: "They hollered at us before the strike and said, 'We're going to do this thing on the inside, and we need your support from the outside'.... They came up with solutions for how to resolve harm and conflict inside, without violence. They won some demands, but they also showed us—if it's possible to do this in solitary, think of what's possible for people in less restrictive conditions."

What's more, many of the same arguments raised against the scourge of solitary can also be used against imprisonment itself, though with different connotations: Isolation, dehumanization, deprivation of contact, and violence are characteristics of incarceration everywhere. And as Isaac mentioned, the strikers' actions—the historic commitment made through the Agreement to End Hostilities, and the project of coordinating nonviolent resistance despite enormous communication barriers—also point to exciting possibilities for resolving harm and conflict *without* (in fact, in spite of) law enforcement and prison.

However, much media coverage reduced the strike's significance to a protest against specific *conditions* alone, creating the illusion that prisons, and even solitary confinement, can be made "humane"—that they are fixable. Suddenly, mainstream voices were issuing calls to cease the "cruel and unusual punishment," pointing to certain brutal practices as "out of the ordinary" modes of discipline. Of course, ameliorating conditions is always an important goal: It's crucial, for example, to provide nutritious food and allow prisoners to call their families. But in framing these improvements as ends in themselves, the terms of "ordinary" punishment are solidified: Caging people is "usual," so it's fine!

Additionally, small concessions are sometimes used to divert attention from larger ongoing injustices. Several months after the 2013 hunger strike, Dolores Canales of California Families to End Solitary Confinement noted in a *MintPress News* interview that, despite a few reforms implemented by the Department of Corrections—such as changes in criteria for placing people in SHUs—the basic picture hadn't changed. "They can still use solitary indefinitely," Canales said. "They don't see a problem with it, with leaving somebody for thirty or forty years in their cell. They won't acknowledge it's a problem."[5]

And so, doing decarceration-focused work means bearing in mind long-term impacts. For instance, California Families to

Abolish Solitary Confinement sets *ending* the practice of isolation as its ultimate goal. And as Black and Pink's mission statement puts it, "Any advocacy, services, organizing and direct action we take will be sure to remove bricks from the system, not put in others we will need to abolish later."

"There's Too Many People in This Prison"

Closing prisons and reducing populations don't blaze a straight path to freedom. It can be jagged. It can be messy. When Illinois Governor Pat Quinn announced in February 2012 that Dwight Correctional Center would be closing along with Tamms, decarceration activists both inside and outside were jubilant. The closing of a prison heralds the possibility of the entire system's crumbling.

But when I received the news of Dwight's closing through an elated press release email from an activist group, my own elation wasn't based on the anti-prison victory alone. It also stemmed from the fact that my sister was living inside that prison.

Dwight served as both Illinois' maximum-security women's prison and also the "intake" center for prisoners newly received into the system. Kayla was holed up in Dwight, waiting to be bussed off to a minimum-security spot a little farther south. Even if they closed Dwight the instant I opened the email, Kayla wouldn't be freed—she would be whisked away to another joint. Still, the image in my mind of the prison shuttering its windows looked something like hope.

A year and a half later, in fall 2013, I reflect on that sense of hope while pacing the waiting room at Logan Prison, impatient to be called in for a visit with my sister. Phones and reading material are prohibited, so people are milling around the vending machine. A hazy tension hovers in the air; we have no idea how long we'll be waiting, and the guards on duty won't drop a clue. One simply says, "There's too many visitors, because there's too many people in this prison."

A short, graying man in a denim shirt who's leaning against the wall near me comments, "I bet you we wait here another hour, two hours. We might not even get in before visiting hours are over, no kidding." Like my family, this man drives four hours to get to Logan, he tells me, sometimes to wait about the same amount of time. When he finally gets in to see his daughter, she says she can't get an appointment with the prison dentist to get a severely aching tooth pulled; the waiting list is too long. I describe the way Kayla has been neglected since giving birth; she's suffering a kidney infection, writhing in pain, with little medical attention.

The man shook his head. "It's been like this ever since they closed down Dwight."

It's not an unheard-of opinion; Dwight's closing wasn't handled well. Before the shutdown, the prison watchdog group John Howard Association warned against rapidly closing Dwight: "Absent a clear plan to reduce population, the shuttering of Dwight is likely to exacerbate crowded conditions [at other prisons], which may further undermine the health, welfare and safety of staff and inmates," the association argued, adding that Logan's location—further from Chicago than Dwight—would make visiting more difficult for most families.[6]

Laurie Jo Reynolds, who helped lead the campaign to close Tamms and also advocated closing Dwight, notes that shutting down a prison isn't always a perfect tactic, nor should it be undertaken unilaterally without consideration for prisoners' well-being. "Some people talk about it as a strategy where you close prisons and then there's overcrowding, and that results in more pressure to reduce prison populations," she says. "But then do you do that on the backs of the people there?"

Closing a prison like Tamms was an unequivocal victory for both the prisoners released from solitary and the overall shrinking of the prison system: The supermax was only half-full, and there were empty cells lying in wait at other men's prisons in the state. By some standards, Dwight was a slightly trickier business. In addition to ensuring care for people involved, Laurie Jo urges that advocacy for prison closings be combined with pushes to reduce populations and change sentencing laws. In other words: Get people out.

Back in the waiting room at Logan, the man in the denim shirt shakes his head. "Six more months for my daughter. Really, I just hope she'll just never come back here. That would solve this whole problem, wouldn't it?"

Getting People Out

How to approach that towering goal of getting people out—and preventing people from going in? Well, if there were a sure way to do it tidily, it might already have been accomplished. As Joseph "Jazz" Hayden, who became an activist while incarcerated and now heads up the New York–based Campaign to End the New Jim Crow (named after Michelle Alexander's book), puts it, "This system of power has a long history, from the genocide of indigenous populations, enslaving Africans, chain gangs, convict lease, now mass incarceration and perpetual punishment and collateral consequences. They're not going to just *let* us take it down."

The answer, says Jazz, must be to chip away at the edifice from many different directions, to unite community groups and build coalitions bent on halting the cycle. Local groups in New Orleans forged such a coalition to challenge that cycle in the wake of tragedy. When Hurricane Katrina hit New Orleans in 2005, it shattered most of the Orleans Parish Prison (OPP), the city's sprawling jail complex, leaving the people inside wading through chest-deep water for hours, awaiting rescue until after the storm was over. The hurricane drew attention to overcrowding and heinous conditions inside the jail, as well as to the racism that drove the system. Eighty-six percent of the people in the jail are black,[7] and the coalition stated, "Subhuman conditions at OPP are intimately tied to the value that we as a city assign to African American life, and our staggering incarceration rate is fundamentally about our society's fear of black people."[8]

And so, at a time when the city could have used the evident "overcrowding" as an excuse to build more space, the Orleans Parish Prison Reform Coalition seized the opportunity to advocate for a cap on the jail population, to force the release of some prisoners and prevent incarcerating new ones. (As Layne Mullett, a cofounder of the Philadelphia-based group Decarcerate PA, notes, "If they build it, they will fill it—and they will probably overfill it.")

The coalition brought together faith communities, ex-prisoner groups, the American Civil Liberties Union, Critical Resistance's New Orleans chapter, BreakOUT! (a group focused on the criminalization of LGBTQ youth), The National Lawyers Guild, and others. They pushed for a 1,438-person jail limit, and for the closing of all other jail buildings into which the city could transfer people.

After years of hosting public comment forums, conducting public education campaigns, holding press conferences, and delivering lengthy petitions to the city council, they won their limit: a city ordinance capping the jail size at 1,438 and mandating the closure of additional jail buildings.

However, says Audrey Stuart, one of the coalition's organizers, "winning" doesn't mean achieving a cap and stepping back. "There have been several recent amendments to the ordinance that have allowed for other buildings to remain open longer than specified," she tells me. "We're working to enforce the cap—and to push for reducing our still extremely high incarceration rate." When it comes to decarceration, a victory is never the end.

Bail and Beyond

The New Orleans coalition's focus addresses a population that often garners less publicity than people serving prison time: the nearly 750,000 people locked up in local jails, many of whom are simply waiting to be tried.[9] A study of people in New York City arrested on nonfelony charges whose bail was set at $1,000 or less showed that 87 percent were in jail because they could not pay the bail amount.[10] People of color are routinely assigned higher bail amounts.[11] An inability to pay bail has reverberating consequences that extend far beyond the pretrial period. Those who are jailed while awaiting trial are more likely to be convicted and more likely to receive long sentences than their bailed-out counterparts, who are able to address their legal charges from within their communities. Plus, people who are jailed before trial may lose their jobs, housing, or custody of their children—and may feel forced to accept a plea bargain just to get out temporarily.[12]

But recently a rare path to release emerged for a nineteen-year-old young man arrested on drug charges in Massachusetts, who was assigned a very low bail but still couldn't pay it. The Massachusetts Bail Fund, a coalition of activists and social workers who fundraise and post bail for folks whose families can't post their own, had recently been born. The fund paid the man's bail, and he was released to a residential drug treatment program with which the fund connected him, Norma Wassel, the organization's founder, tells me. Six months later, when his case reached its final hearing, the district attorney stated that through his progress in treatment, "The defendant showed me that he could stay out of trouble and get the help he needed." Not only had this young man been spared six months of pretrial incarceration, but he'd also been granted the chance to help shape his own post-hearing future.

Groups doing other types of prisoner advocacy can cast a line out to the Massachusetts Bail Fund for help. Jason Lydon of Black and Pink says, "Working with them, we've been able to save people from many months in jail awaiting trial, and save some from getting sentenced to jail time at all, as they show up in court out of chains." The fund also actively advocates for moving away from cash bail toward release and community accountability, in which services are provided by organizations based within the community instead of by state agencies—removing bricks instead of adding them.

Activism around bail, which usually happens in close collaboration with the person inside whose bail is being targeted, can serve another important decarcerative function. In lots of cases in which national campaigns have sprouted up around particular people standing trial, raising bail money is a dynamic step toward broader organizing and action. Consider Marissa Alexander, who was charged with aggravated assault with a deadly weapon for firing a warning shot to stave off an attack from her abusive husband, or Shanesha Taylor, charged with felony child abuse for leaving her kids in the car while interviewing for a job. Public campaigns to raise bail and/or legal expenses for them have exponentially raised the profiles of their cases—and raised awareness of the issues from which those cases stem: the criminalization of black domestic violence survivors, for example, or the utter void of support provided for poor, unemployed moms of color.

Of course, campaigns to end the confinement of certain prisoners—and thus draw attention to the social forces that ground and uphold the system—don't stop at (or necessarily start at) fundraising. The ongoing movements to free political prisoners like Leonard Peltier, Mumia Abu-Jamal, Albert Woodfox, Herman Bell, Russell "Maroon" Shoatz, Mondo we Langa, and many, many others continue to highlight the intertwined forces of racism and suppression of political resistance that power the criminal punishment machine.

The family-led fights to win clemency for prisoners such as Tyrone Brown—a seventeen-year-old incarcerated on a life sentence for smoking pot while on probation—and Richard Paey, a man who suffered from MS, sentenced to twenty-five years for using painkillers prescribed by his doctor—began to throw the drug war into a ghastly light, even for some of the most tenacious proponents of "Just Say No." And recently, the movements to support women such as Marissa Alexander, Shanesha Taylor, CeCe McDonald (a trans woman convicted of stabbing an attacker in self-defense), and many others have become freedom campaigns in many senses of the word. They're geared toward all-out release, but also toward a wider understanding of who is denied freedom: freedom from incarceration, freedom from gender violence, freedom from police violence, freedom from poverty, freedom from oppression.

Decarceration Nation

Lillie Branch-Kennedy of Richmond, Virginia, didn't encounter the matrix of the criminal punishment system by choice. "I wish from the bottom of my heart that I never had to learn firsthand about America's world record for mass incarceration, and about Virginia's criminal system that targets and ensnares young black men," says Lillie, who founded the Resource Information Help for the Disadvantaged (RIHD), an advocacy group for Virginia prisoners and their families. Sixty-one percent of state prisoners are black; for every white person incarcerated in Virginia, six black people are behind bars.[13] That number includes Lillie's son Donald.

In 2001, Donald—who was attending Virginia State on a scholarship but had recently begun "running with the wrong crowd"—was arrested as an accessory to a robbery. For a crime that would ordinarily carry a sentence of 3 to 8 years, Donald was sentenced to 127.

As the summer before his junior year of college wound to an end, instead of returning to school, Donald was bussed off to prison: Wallens Ridge, a supermax in the Appalachian mountains, a steep eight-hour drive from Lillie's home. With her son caged in twenty-three-hour-a-day lockdown and her life pinned to the commute to see him, Lillie couldn't ignore the system. So she decided to take it on.

In addition to coordinating transportation for prisoners' family members (providing monthly van trips to four Virginia state prisons), Lillie steered RIHD toward decarceration advocacy, traveling the state to rally family members against various manifestations of the prison-industrial complex, from "ban the box" campaigns (eliminating criminal background questions from initial employment forms) to ending mandatory-minimum sentencing to bringing back parole, which has been abolished in Virginia since 1995. Lillie's not timid about her commitment to broad-scale decarceration; she rejects a recent Virginia bill aimed at reinstating parole for people convicted of nonviolent crimes only, which entrenches a sort of "good prisoner vs. bad prisoner" mentality. "It's unfair and discriminatory," she says.

Lillie knows that no single group can triumph over the prison nation—and RIHD isn't going it alone. It's part of a growing coalition of local campaigns called Nation Inside, which is sweeping the country by way of ground-level activism, Facebook, Twitter, email, blogs, "storybanks," petitions, and a multifaceted website where new efforts are continually sprouting up.

It all started around the time Donald was incarcerated in 2001. Many of the prisoners at Wallens Ridge were listening to a hip-hop show called "Holler to the Hood," launched by artist-activists Nick Szuberla and Amelia Kirby to serve the populations of central Appalachia's prisons. "It was meant to culturally acknowledge the fact that there were folks being shipped into the region," Nick tells me. Indeed, many people in these Appalachia coalfield prisons hailed from far-flung states—New Mexico, Connecticut, Wyoming. Many were people of color from urban areas, plunked down in a white, rural landscape. Soon, Nick says, prisoners began writing into the show, describing abuse by guards, the brutal conditions of their confinement, and their isolation from loved ones far away. Not long after, prisoners' families began calling in, using the program to speak directly to their loved ones. Lillie Branch-Kennedy was one of those callers.

"From there," Nick says, "people like Lillie started to use the show as an organizing tool. Family members laid the foundation for an organizing effort that went beyond the station." Ironically, because the Appalachian prisons drew their populations from such disparate parts of the country, the radio show's potential as a tool for activism was hugely amplified: Families in Virginia were linking up with families in Connecticut, New Mexico, and Washington, D.C., sowing seeds for a national network. Like Lillie, family members in other states were launching campaigns from the ground up, working with the support of their network to confront the urgent issues they witnessed—and felt—firsthand. They began to meet each year in person: a coalition of about forty people, geographically scattered but bound by shared pain and conviction. In late 2011, the coalition gave itself its name, Nation Inside—it refers to the "nation inside of our nation," a prison population the size of some countries—and committed to building an online platform that would draw together grassroots, local campaigns like theirs: communities challenging the systems that fuel incarceration.

Prisoners wrote the press releases, drew the artwork, and collaborated in laying the plans that launched the coalition, which now unites more than 125,000 people and thirty groups, from a New York campaign working for the release of aging prisoners to a group fighting to stop the construction of a jail in Illinois' Champaign County to an Oregon-based campaign calling for divestment from private prison companies.

Charting these kinds of networks, crossing neighborhood lines and state lines and the walls of prison, is not just preparation for decarceration; it is part of the work of decarceration itself. Making connections means refusing to isolate, to ignore, to hide, to replicate the patterns of the prison. It means refusing to be canceled.

Beware the Women's Villages

Over the past several years, the raised voices of anti-prison activists and scholars, coupled with the tightening of state budgets, have resulted in a shocking shift: Prison populations have slowly begun to decrease nationwide. Mainstream media outlets now regularly condemn the drug war and excoriate vile prison conditions. Laurie Jo Reynolds from the Tamms campaign tells me, "Six years ago, you'd say 'solitary confinement,' and nobody knew what it was! Now my accountant is making small talk about solitary." But, she notes, that doesn't mean most people are making larger talk about the place of prison in our politics, economy, and culture.

As Mariame Kaba from Project NIA notes in a piece called "Prison Reform Is in Vogue ... and Other Strange Things": "Absent the large-scale, cross-sectional movement-building needed in order to uproot the oppressions that both give rise to the PIC and hold it in place, I'm afraid that this latest round of proposed prison reforms will only be another version of tinkering towards imperfection."[14]

That tinkering is happening from a variety of directions—including from within the criminal punishment system itself. Look at a prison website these days and you may not realize it's a prison. Boasting of dog-training programs, culinary arts classes, cosmetology, "cake decorating" seminars, and an array of "volunteering opportunities," many never use the word "prison" in their publicity materials, opting instead for the innocuous term "facility." Isaac Ontiveros points out, "Massive numbers of dollars still go toward building new cages to target poor black and brown people, but they take up the language of reform, saying things like, 'We're going to provide "women's villages" with services for underserved women of color'—this kinder, gentler rhetoric."

Diana Zuñiga, the statewide field organizer of the forty-organization-strong decarceration coalition Californians United for a Responsible Budget (CURB), talks of how policies that expand the prison nation creep in under the guise of confronting mass incarceration. In California, the state is carrying out a process of "realignment," shifting large numbers of incarcerated people from prisons to county jails. The strategy, championed as a route to reducing the state's skyrocketing prison budget and ending the "revolving door" of recidivism,[15] has actually resulted in most counties moving toward jail expansion.[16] Diana is often alarmed to hear CURB's calls for shrinking the prison system echoed by officials calling for "mental health jails" and "social service jails." She says, "We have seen our language be coopted so that law enforcement can appear to be doing the 'right thing.'"

Diana is pointing to an even more insidious recent trend in addition to the production of "alternative" forms of confinement: A wide range of influential political groups, switching from a push for "tough on crime" legislation to a "right on crime" message, are advocating that money saved from reducing prison populations be spent on heightened policing and surveillance. The Texas-based conservative group Right on Crime touts "reforms" like increasing monitoring and records-keeping on formerly incarcerated people, scaling up the use of private security companies, and zeroing in on "crime hotspots" in cities: poor neighborhoods of color.[17]

I broach the subject with Jazz from the Campaign to End the New Jim Crow, who's also the organizer behind Cop Watch, a group that videotapes police searching, harassing, and beating people. He's also been a leader in the struggle to end New York's "stop and frisk" policy. Jazz points to the way that "targeted" policing tends to play out in reality: violence directed at neighborhoods of color, especially black neighborhoods. "Turning our communities into open-air prisons is not the solution to violence," he says.

Where *will* we turn to deal with violence, harm, and conflict in a landscape that's not fashioned around incarceration? Since right now, prison is society's go-to "solution," thinking beyond the prison means not only uprooting it, but also offering new answers to harm. Layne from Decarcerate PA articulates it like this: "Abolition is a complicated goal which involves tearing down one world and building another."

They're interconnected, of course—the communities and strategies and visions concocted while doing the "tearing down" provide a glimpse of that world beyond prisons. As the Pelican Bay prisoners demonstrated, strategies for connection and inter-relation, for staving off harm and violence, can be forged mightily while straining against thick walls of injustice. But no matter how you swing it, decarceration comes with a healthy share of unpredictability. Without prescribed, violently enforced systems dictating how we move through the world, we'll need to come together and pave our own roads forward. And they won't always be smooth and clear.

Chapter 8

Telling Stories

"We need to trust people to be the experts on their own lives."
—*Domestic violence survivor interviewed by the*
Story Telling & Organizing Project

Although Angelica's entrance into the world undoubtedly ranks as my family's most significant event of 2013, followed by Kayla's reincarceration, the loss of a dearly loved inanimate object nears the top of my Big Deal list. On a sleepy late summer evening shortly before my sister gives birth, I'm ambling across the parking lot of a Seattle restaurant late in the evening with two old friends. We're relishing the warm breeze and chatting about the possibility of ice cream.

But one of my companions stops short, two feet from my car.

"Oh my *God*," she says, low. "The window." The back window has been shattered through the middle, as if by a bowling ball. Glistening shards are still dropping lightly onto the back seat.

My heart thuds, pushes me forward. I plunge my hand through the hole. "Where is my laptop?" I say, patting the shard-covered seat, then pounding it. The sharp bits stick to my palm, which emerges wet and red-slitted. The laptop—along with the uncomfortable shoulder bag in which it was kept, which also contained my only pair of glasses, an assortment of tampons, and a notepad filled with embarrassingly moonlike self-portraits sketched during a PowerPoint presentation at a recent conference—is nowhere. The back seat is empty.

One hundred thousand words of the book I've been researching and writing for the last eleven months, about prison and prisoners and, well, "crime," are stored inside that computer. It also contains millions more cherished words—stories, articles, notes, humiliating diary entries from my early twenties, passwords "hidden" in the guise of other files—and all the music I've acquired since 2004. My many un-Facebooked photos. My book, my book.

"Do you have it backed up?" my friend's voice floats into my ear, as if traveling down from the tree. No. I *have* an external hard drive—I've had it for seven months. I just haven't yet removed it from its packaging.

You aren't supposed to leave your laptop on the car seat. I have never left my laptop on the car seat, always stowing it away securely in a corner of the trunk. But tonight, I did.

I think fleetingly of the person who bashed in the window. I wonder what they must have been thinking in the act of bashing, whether they needed money, whether they were just teenagers trying to be badass, whether they had thought of me, whether they were thinking about me now. In the background, someone murmurs something about a police report. Calls are made on a cell phone, the name of the restaurant given, the make and model of the car.

"They've got your phone number," I'm told. "We gave them the info about your case, so they're on it." In my head, a page from the book I've lost reads itself to me, slowly. One sentence asks, "Before you call the police, think, are they really going to help—and who are they going to hurt?" Another reasonably points out, "The prison-industrial complex deals with 'cases,' instead of 'problems' and 'human beings.'"

I grab for my phone. My palms are still wet, dotted with small red cuts. I stare at my phone, willing the police to call.

But over the next week, I wait and wait for the announcement of the triumphant return of my laptop. The police never locate it. My "case" is tucked into a bulging file with hundreds of other sorrowful, identical tales—dozens of stolen-laptop reports have already been filed in Seattle that summer. ("It's kind of an epidemic!" one officer explains to me excitedly over the phone.) Arrests—probably of poor people and people of color—are undoubtedly made as a result of some of those stories. Some of those arrested are probably sent to prison, and some of them may not be guilty. When they get out of prison, it remains to be seen whether they'll steal more laptops. Or rather, it remains to *not* be seen. I'll certainly never know.

In fact, the process I bought into provided no support for me, beyond the false, momentary sense of security that came from filing a report. It was geared toward catching and punishing a person—or a bunch of people—rather than addressing the impact of my loss, or the causes of the "epidemic" in the first place. It's just one component of a system obsessed not with solving problems or aiding victims, but with "crime."

What's Crime?

Under a framework based on "crime," a person's relationship to the *law*—not to other people—determines whether they have done something wrong. As soon as I pull out my notepad to interview Mariame Kaba of Project NIA, she tells me she's not going to use the word "crime." She clarifies, "We use the word 'harm.'

The question is, 'What have you done to someone else? How have you harmed another person?'"

The stealing of a laptop may violate a law, but the real reason it's bad is because it hurt me. "Harm" is not always equivalent to the things the state considers crime.

It gets trickier. "Many things create harm that aren't legally crimes," Mariame says, and points to the kinds of business transactions that wreak havoc on the poor. From the genocide of Native peoples in the US and Canada to the rampant practice of wage theft against low-income workers to the construction of carcinogenic factories in poor people's backyards to the profits reaped by the private prison industry at the expense of millions of lives, accountability-free forms of robbery and murder abound. Indeed, nonviolence activist Kathy Kelly writes in her post-incarceration memoir *Other Lands Have Dreams*: "What actions pose the greatest threats to US people and to the survival of our planet? Topping any rational list would be the development, storage, sale and threatened use of nuclear weapons, along with the stockpiling and use of chemical, biological and conventional weapons." These are not classified as *crimes* under law, but they cause massive harm—the most massive harm.

Lacino Hamilton, who's serving a life sentence in Michigan, writes to me about the hazy definition of crime. He questions why accepted models for measuring crime, such as the Department of Justice's Uniform Crime Report, don't include colonial, economic, political, international, and environmental violence, even when that violence kills vast numbers of people. "To pass these statistics off as anything other than a very narrow investigation of poor and oppressed people is a crime of sorts," Lacino writes. Conversely, plenty of things that it would be tough to frame as *harm* are classified as crimes, punishable by law, especially if you're a person of color: undocumented immigration, drug possession, sex work, debt.

This issue of defining and assessing the value of the "crime" label is critical in the quest for "solutions." If continuing to be black or brown or poor or gender-nonconforming results in future prison time, then no amount of "rehabilitation" is going to do the trick. As Angela Davis has written, "One has a greater chance of going to jail or prison if one is a young black man than if one is an actual law-breaker."[1] And as Glenn E. Martin tells me of the primarily black and brown population with which his organization works, "Some of our clients could get arrested for dropping their MetroCard in the subway, for looking at someone the wrong way." In fact, a 2011 study by the Illinois Disproportionate Justice Impact Study Commission found that, for low-level drug possession charges, black people were almost five times more likely to be sentenced to prison as white people convicted of the same crime. For *all* crimes, black people were almost twice as likely to be prosecuted than white people, with Latinos 1.4 times as likely as white people to be prosecuted.[2] When we look at how the word "crime" is used to crush lives and hurt communities and worsen already painful situations, it ceases to be useful for talking about transformation.

Moving in a direction that drops prison as the go-to solution to pain or violence, I'll use the word "harm" to refer to that pain or violence, unless I'm talking about a law-based situation that requires the use of "crime." This is for accuracy's sake, but it will also serve to put the focus on what's happening to the people involved—and the victim or survivor's right to heal—as opposed to the "breaking" of a law. A law can't really get hurt, and it doesn't feel pain when it breaks.

"Hurt People Hurt People"

"Crime" seems straightforward: It's a violation of a law, which is spelled out on paper. "Harm" is more messy, more tangled because it is humanly, instead of legally, determined. People can't be clearly split and categorized by "guilt" and "innocence," by "bad" and "good," or even, sometimes, by "perpetrator" and "victim." People who do great damage have, usually, been profoundly injured themselves. The roots of harm-doing are knotted and deep. Mariame tells me, "Hurt people hurt people."

My pen pal Lacino has been incarcerated for two decades, since the age of nineteen. Locked up for homicide, he has always contested his conviction (which is based on the testimony of one informant who was granted a reduced sentence after testifying against Lacino and others). Lacino reached out to me through a prominent activist who is pushing for a retrial of his case. He considers his incarceration a "crime," but says it is not out of place in the progression of his life: a snarled sequence of received and inflicted harms.

Lacino's mother gave birth to him at the age of fourteen while she was a ward of the state. Lacino was placed in foster care himself for three and a half years and then returned to his mother—but she abandoned him after a few days, leaving him stranded at a bake sale. She was poor, suffering from crack dependency, and, Lacino says, "barely surviving." Lacino spent the next couple of years jumping from foster home to foster home. Soon after he turned five, he was placed with a long-term foster family—the people he'd live with for the next six years. While the Michigan Department of Human Services approved of the situation's permanence and the family's relative financial stability, Lacino describes those years as "slavery." His foster parents put him to work on a near-constant regimen of household labor. They routinely withheld meals and denied him new clothing as he grew, though they regularly bought new clothes for themselves. He tells of how, several times a week, they whipped him with a belt as he lay face-down on his bed, naked.

At the age of eleven, Lacino put his foot down. He left home and began living on the street, where he stole in order to eat and slept in stolen cars. There, theft and violence were not only normal, they were the prescription for staying alive. "My de facto family became the people I met in the streets—other black youth close to me in age, who, like myself, were fleeing dysfunctional living arrangements," Lacino writes to me, going on to say that these relationships, adrift on constantly changing currents of circumstance, were not lasting ones. From the familial level to the community level to their relations with the larger world, "Our entire lives were modeled and based on alienation." For these kids, stealing and fighting were justifiable not only because they were means of survival, but also because they were the ways of life they'd always known.

A Queensland, Australia, study showed that people who were physically abused as children were much more likely to offend later on.[3] (The study didn't account for verbal and psychological harm, or the constant, sustained abuse of poverty, institutional racism, heterosexism, ableism, and other factors.) And according to the National Council on Crime and Delinquency, the number one indicator for whether teenagers engage in "criminal behavior" is whether or not they've been victims of crime themselves.[4] Glenn E. Martin tells me, "Most people who appear in court were themselves victims at some point. But no one in court would know it."

Community Justice

One framework that aims to center human beings—to look at harms not as legal violations, but as problems that occur between people—is called restorative justice (RJ). Many of the restorative justice model's principles have emerged from widespread indigenous practices that have been overwhelmingly dismissed by modern Western systems of power. Instead of exacting revenge, restorative justice's goals are to build relationships, empower victims, support them in their healing processes, help them call out the behaviors of those who have harmed them, and bolster them in asking for the things they need to move on. Restorative justice strategies ideally also aim to guide people who have done harm in making reparations to victims (depending on the situation), making substantive changes that help prevent future harm, and staying accountable for keeping up those new behaviors.[5]

A standard restorative justice response to harm is a "peace circle," which brings together victims, the people who've done harm, families of each, and community members (or some combination of these), with the goal of working toward understanding, healing, and, in many cases, reconciliation and reparations. The circle—or the series of circles it may take to reach a resolution—may conclude with an "accountability agreement," a consensus statement for moving forward. Often, these circles also help to forge new relationships and new understandings. In a peace circle, I could, theoretically, meet the person who stole my laptop and convey the long-lasting ways in which the theft hurt me.

Another framework that steps outside the PIC mentality is transformative justice, which overlaps with restorative justice in some ways. It focuses on promoting healing for survivors, accountability for people who harm, and a collectively safer and more connected community. But—especially when it comes to sexual and domestic violence—it also calls into question the concept of "restoration," which can assume that there's a good place in the past to return to. Transformative justice strongly emphasizes "transformation of the social conditions that perpetuate violence—systems of oppression and exploitation, domination, and state violence," according to Generation FIVE, an advocacy organization dedicated to ending the sexual abuse of children through transformative means.[6]

When applied to a specific harm or conflict, the emphasis of transformative justice is often on long-term change-making, addressing behaviors and ways of occupying the world, as opposed to exacting a resolution to one incident. Transformative justice generally operates wholly separate from the state, while restorative justice sometimes works in tandem with police departments, serving as an "alternative to incarceration." Grounded in principles of connection, both of these community-based practices are very different from the standard practices of a courtroom.

"Justice" for Victims and Families

Ricky Joseph Langley was charged with the capital murder of a six-year-old boy in Louisiana in 1994. Nine years later, in a retrial, the prosecutor working on the case was intent on seeking the death penalty. The victim's mother, however, vehemently opposed the execution of the man who had killed her son. The death of this man would do nothing to allay her grief, she said, especially since it would be preceded by the anguish of another long murder trial—an impediment to healing. She pleaded with the lawyer, asking him not to pursue a sentence of death.

The prosecutor grew furious with her noncompliance. He "even blamed [the mother], in part, for the jury's verdict of second-degree murder—a verdict that does not permit the death penalty," according to legal scholar and prosecutor Angela J. Davis (not to be confused with Angela Y. Davis, activist and author of *Are Prisons Obsolete?*), recounting the case in *Arbitrary Justice.* As the pursuit of capital punishment pushed forward, the boy's mother expressed that the prosecutor had made her life even more painful in the wake of her son's death.[7]

In court, questions are focused on the people accused of doing harm: whether to punish them, and then how much to punish them. Victims and survivors—especially, Davis notes, poor people and people of color—are tossed to the sidelines, rendered powerless. Their wishes are rarely spotlighted in the courtroom except when they make juicy TV fodder—for instance, a high-profile murder case in which a victim's family member announces that the defendant should "rot in jail" or die, in order to "see justice served." It's not just people who've done harm who are isolated by the prison-industrial complex. It's victims, communities, and families, too.

In a journal entry she shares with me from 2005, when Kayla was heading to juvenile detention, Mom writes: "Now the courts are involved, and I stand before the judge and watch him not even glance at me let alone consult me. It is out of my hands. You can't say a word, and if you do, you're considered to be disrupting the court."

A community-based justice approach ideally acknowledges the complex ways in which conflicts affect families, and engages them in the processes of justice and healing. Including the community also helps place an incident in the context of what *else* is going on—how the particular act in question fits with larger trends in the neighborhood, the town, the county, the world.

A Shifted Approach to Life

For Flathead County, Montana, a working-class, majority-Republican locale at the edge of Glacier National Park, it was numbers that prompted a turn toward restorative justice.[8] The county's wakeup call was a 2009 University of Montana study of "juvenile offender status," which awarded it the dubious honor of holding the highest youth recidivism rate in the state.[9]

At the time, Flathead's approach to juvenile justice involved spending loads of money removing kids from their homes and placing them in detention centers. This program of cutting kids off from their families and communities wasn't doing the trick. "At-risk teens are in a really unique place in that they already feel disconnected from society because of their age/development status," Kate Berry, who works with Flathead's current restorative justice program, tells me. "This is only exacerbated by the fact that they have committed an offense that further alienates them from their communities." If they're incarcerated, they're isolated even further.

Nowadays, in Flathead County, *all* victims of youth crime are engaged in a process that moves toward a "victim-offender" circle, if they so choose.[*] The town didn't attempt to build a restorative justice program inside the police department (a not-uncommon

---

[*] Many restorative justice programs begin with youth, especially if they operate within dominant society; it's simply less controversial as public policy. Hopefully, restorative justice leaders tell me, the youth program will model the ways in which the process can function, which will be useful for an expansion of adult-based efforts down the line. Also, youth crime comprises a significant chunk of crime, and it's important to address that behavior early: Most ex-prisoners under forty years old recidivate, most over fifty-five don't. Also, after they reach twenty-five, we see a steep drop in offenses. Still, Father David Kelly hopes that restorative efforts will soon expand to include older people. He explains to me that after working with thousands of children and adults bound up in the criminal "justice" system, he's always struck by the fact that the adults are, well, more *mature*, more likely to concede when they're not thinking right, less likely to act out during the process. "Anyone can change," he says.

move in line with the "right on crime" approach, which can actually serve to bolster the prison-industrial complex by expanding the range of what constitutes policing). Instead, the probation department handed the reins to the Center for Restorative Youth Justice (CRYJ), a separate organization that holds circles, runs a "community accountability board" that meets with youth to discuss the impact of their behavior on their community, organizes a community service program, and provides spaces for accountability-oriented dialogue around drugs and alcohol.

It's important to note that CRYJ can't control who gets arrested and why. Police still exist in Flathead County, along with the profound problems embedded in that institution. It's the juvenile probation department that calls CRYJ when a kid gets in trouble. Despite this inherent dissonance, the center strives to maintain a commitment to principles of transformation: It emphasizes forging new community bonds (it doesn't keep to the mold of "restoring" old ones) and recognizing the larger issues of social injustice that shape kids' motivations.

Once the program took hold, it took off. The county docked a 13 percent recidivism rate in 2011, in contrast with the state's youth recidivism rate of 46 percent.[10] The numerical improvement is encouraging, but the folks I speak with in Flathead County agree that the most important "measurements" are the new relationships that are created: the strengthened community and the previously nonexistent bonds that were formed. Victims have responded positively as well. Bill Emerson, the victim of a residential break-in, says of the conference he and his wife had with the youth ("Just a kid!" he comments) who did it: "I can't tell you how much going through the conference meant to us. Had we not, I fear we may have never really put that incident to rest."

One CRYJ social worker shares with me a small story that illustrates that community strengthening: Recently, a youth stole and destroyed a commercial painter's vehicle, which contained most of the equipment and supplies that were vital to the man's business. The painter spoke to the youth, recounting the impact of the theft and destruction on his business, how his employees were unable to work and lost pay until he could buy a new vehicle. The painter's wife then told how the incident occurred in late November, creating an instant host of financial woes and leaving them unable to buy Christmas gifts for their kids. The youth expressed deep remorse and agreed to pay restitution money, which he would earn. The painter and his wife then reached out further, telling the youth that he was a valued member of the community, and that if he stayed on track they would give him a job. In addition, they asked that the youth write them a monthly letter detailing his progress.

Diane Dwyer, CRYJ's victim impact coordinator who leads the circle-based aspect of the program, said of the youth in this case: "He was so taken with their benevolence.... This adolescent had several other offenses before he did this. He had very little supervision at home and took pride in being an 'offender' till this happened." So far, she says, the youth has moved forward with his monthly letters, developing a strong relationship with the victims, his future employers.

He took pride in being an "offender" until this happened. This change in course, not only in action but also in mindset, is not deterrence. It's not I-really-want-to-do-this-bad-thing-but-I-won't-because-I'll-get-arrested (which, of course, in a retribution-oriented system, is a less likely sentiment than I'm-going-to-do-this-bad-thing-and-try-not-to-get-caught). This is a shifted approach to life.

Several years ago in Flathead County, a fifteen-year-old kid crashed a car and killed a young woman in her twenties. The woman's parents, although—or perhaps because—they were awash in grief, very much wanted to engage in a restorative process. This tragedy could have resulted in a stint in juvie, a "graduation" to adult prison, and, quite possibly, future harm. Instead, a circle was organized, including the driver and his friends, the deceased woman's parents, the highway patrol officer at the scene, and passersby who stopped to assist after the accident.

No one went to jail. After an intensive series of circles in which the deceased woman's parents described what they would need to begin healing, an accountability agreement was reached. As part of that agreement, the youth developed an informational pamphlet regarding the risks of teen driving and the consequences of carelessness on the road and presented it at area schools, along with the story of what he did. Instead of being siphoned off from his community and sent to prison and forgotten, the driver of that car became a spokesperson for road awareness and caution, striving to prevent others from making the dangerous choices he had made, inflicting the immense harm he had inflicted. Real justice isn't *only* about preventing people from doing wrong. It's about supporting them in doing right.

Decriminalizing Remorse

There's an essential ingredient that sits at the heart of this different approach to justice: remorse. The role of remorse in court is often simply just that—a "role" that's played by defendants, coached by their lawyers once they're entering a guilty plea, in order to appeal to the judge or jury for a mitigated sentence, or to appeal to parole boards who may cruelly deny release based on a perceived "lack of remorse." In criminal court, an apology isn't addressed to the victim, since the victim usually isn't even present; it's an offering to the judge, a form of self-defense.[11] If a defendant were to reach across the aisle and ask the victim for an honest, repentance-oriented conversation, sans judge, chances are the courtroom would fly into chaos.

When I raise this topic with Father David Kelly, a longtime Chicago youth restorative justice leader who works with people trapped in the system, he speaks of the way the court system explicitly discourages and even punishes such emotion. "As far as expressing remorse, the criminal justice system says *don't* do it," he tells me. "The whole system is designed to say, 'Don't admit anything. You have the right to remain silent. Plead the Fifth.' Father Kelly describes the case of a kid he's working with who's currently in juvenile detention. In court, the kid was desperate to apologize to his victim, but his lawyer told him, "Don't you dare!" Lo and behold, when the sentence came down, the judge scolded the kid for not being remorseful. "He was remorseful," Father Kelly says, "but there was no mechanism for him to show that. He was supposed to be thinking, 'I'm fighting this case they've got against *me.*'" Because "true remorse" can't be expressed, because the legal process is about people defending themselves against the state, there's not much room for accountability to other people.

Carlos Rodriguez, a Chicago-based addiction counselor who works with kids and adults embroiled in the criminal justice system, specializes in community-based and nonadversarial justice. Carlos runs wilderness trips that mesh with these techniques, aiming for 24/7 immersion in healthy, interdependence-based existence. He works to guide people, he says, toward the Mayan principle of *Lak'ech*: "I am the other you, and you are the other me." When we meet for coffee, he tells me how, since these practices are *so* different from the dominant model, it often takes a mental leap to get to a place where real, heartfelt apologies are OK. He describes how in a circle it's necessary to get "out of your head and into your heart," where empathy is born.

"*That* Is Justice!"

Even the most genuine empathy can't erase poverty, racism, and other structural factors that often drive harm. However, Father Kelly points out that empowering people to speak to their daily struggles holds potential for beginning to confront the oppressions that saturate and fuel those struggles. He tells of one circle in which a victim became a mentor to the young man who had burglarized his house. The victim talked passionately about how he'd lived in the house since childhood, and how, in the wake of the break-in, that haven had turned into a space of fear, unsteadiness, and violation for him, his wife, and his two small children. The young man responded with visible sympathy. Then, bolstered by his mother sitting next to him, he told of his past—the traumas he'd endured, the dead weight of poverty that had dragged him backward at every turn.

"When the guy who did the harm was telling his story, the victim felt like, 'Wait a second, this is just like me,'" Father Kelly recalls. "There was a real connectedness." When the group, which included several other members of the community, asked the victim what he needed to help address the harm, he could barely speak—he was so moved by the young man's story. At first, he said he didn't need anything. But then he paused. "Hold on," he said. "There is something I need. This kid has to go back to school."

The return wasn't a simple prospect. The young man had long since dropped out, and the high school didn't want him back. The circle crept toward a stalemate. Then one of the community members, a retired principal, spoke up: "I can help you get back into school." She initiated the process, creating the circumstances through which the young man could keep himself accountable for what he'd done—and, in the process, transform his life.

The connection-building process spun forward, gaining momentum. The victim was a basketball coach, and through ongoing circle conversation he discovered that the young man who'd burglarized his house loved basketball and played often. He'd always wanted to be on a team, but had figured that he'd lost his chance when he left school. Father Kelly recounts how, after a few more conversations, the victim said, "Look. You play basketball, I coach basketball. Would you be willing to come play basketball for my team—and I'll be your mentor?"

The boy agreed. He returned to high school and became an avid basketball player. Years later, his bond with his coach and mentor remains tight.

"Now, *that*!" exclaims Father Kelly. "*That* is justice!"

Reknitting Stories

Still, justice doesn't always look the same, and it may not involve reconciliation. Sometimes, coming face-to-face with a perpetrator (even to receive an apology) may not be something the victim or survivor wants; in fact, regardless of preparation, it may be re-traumatizing. As Philly Stands Up!—an organization that works specifically with perpetrators of sexual assault—notes, "It is not the work of a survivor to hold a perpetrator accountable."[12]

Pointing to the necessity of offering support to victims without urging the goal of reconciliation, Father Kelly speaks of a woman whose two sons were killed within two months of each other. When she first engaged with the circle process, she couldn't speak at all. It took many months of counseling, as well as circles with other mothers who had lost their children, for her to piece together the stories that described her pain: "who she was" before-hand, her personal story, how the series of unspeakable traumas she had borne had ripped her to the core. What she needed was the support of those with shared experiences. "This is about storytelling," Kelly says, describing how trauma is processed in ways that break up our narratives so they often don't seem to make sense. "Narrative helps us to reknit our lives."

These words apply to people who have done harm, as well: Kelly works to guide people who have hurt others toward addressing the ways that *they* have been hurt—the root causes of their harm-doing—so they can be fully accountable for what they've done. In a letter to me, Lacino notes that those who do harm aren't only dealing with the trauma that led up to the act—they're also likely dealing with the trauma of having *done* harm, which may prevent them from confronting what they've done head-on.

This is especially true if they've already been subject to state-inflicted violence like incarceration. "There is no way you can feel good about yourself and do crime," Lacino says. "Something inside of us has to be comatose or dead to harm people and sleep good at night." In order to fuel transformation, he argues, people who have done harm must come to a point where they are revived from that "comatose" state—where they can talk about what has hurt them in the past and what they have done to hurt others.

However, Father Kelly emphasizes, community justice should not be about excusing injustice or letting perpetrators "off the hook." An *effective* community-based process is often a more challenging undertaking than the punitive, isolative one. And it may last a long, long while. "This process is an investment of time and energy," Mariame Kaba says, noting that receiving punishment doesn't take much emotional excavation. "It's not just about The

People Vs. the Perpetrator. It's about forcing you to engage in ways that the current system doesn't." When it comes to reaching inside, yanking out your deepest self and linking it with other people's deepest selves, you can't just go through the motions. Mariame also notes, regarding restorative justice, that sitting in a circle by itself won't lead to long-term shifts in consciousness. It depends on what specific actions are taken, what happens afterward, whether self-conceptions and worldviews are shifted to the point that lasting change can emerge.

Restoring to What?

Mariame points out that, absent the buy-in of all parties involved—and an extremely supportive community and culture—the concept of "restorative justice" can sometimes fall flat. The word "restore" may assume that there's already a "store," a safe and healthy place to return to that can be repaired and peacefully reinhabited. Depending on the practice, it may operate on the premise that relationships can be "repaired," that they were "good" before they were "broken," that a supportive community once existed and can now be fixed. And, by itself, the concept doesn't encompass the huge structural factors (race-, class-, gender- and sexuality-based oppression, to name a few) that drive the system and inhibit "repairs."

Especially when it comes to sexual and domestic violence, the prospect of community "restoration" may well ring discordantly. For survivors of gender violence, the key factor in whether a restorative justice process can be effective is whether a community unites with the victim in holding the perpetrator accountable. Often, communities end up siding with the perpetrator, according to Andrea Smith, a feminist scholar, antiviolence activist, and cofounder of INCITE!: Women of Color Against Violence. Victims and survivors may be coerced into participating in a "restoration" in order to maintain some façade of community equilibrium.

"Restorative justice tends to promote a romanticized notion of community," Andrea tells me. "What if the community is sexist, and racist, and homophobic? Or what if there isn't any community to begin with?" And since practices classified as restorative justice often work with or within the criminal punishment system nowadays, they're controlled by that system's power structures and are subject to its rules.

Being Jazzy

Transformative justice, as distinguished from restorative justice, was first conceived as a response to the ineffectiveness and brutality of the criminal punishment system's methods of dealing with sexual and domestic violence, as well as the way in which restorative justice strategies can betray and further traumatize survivors if the community involved doesn't stand with them. Transformative justice centralizes the "safety, healing, and agency" of survivors; the role of the community is to support them in those goals. Coming back to Generation FIVE's definition of transformative justice—"transforming the social conditions that perpetuate violence," including domination, exploitation, and oppression by the state—the question becomes this: How can we imagine ourselves beyond any sort of prescribed system?

Since it's impossible for *any* readymade model for dealing with violence to work effectively in every single community, Andrea Smith suggests, "We need to be jazzy—to think, in every specific context, what is the perpetrator motivated by?" Like jazz music, transformative justice requires both improvisation and structure. It requires intuition, creativity, collaboration, and an understanding that no process is ever *finished*.

However, just because every situation is different doesn't mean strategies can't be shared. Circles aren't the only places that storytelling can happen, and communities engaged in transformative justice come together through meetings, conferences, online networks, workshops, social media, and spur-of-the-moment conversations to speak about what has worked, what hasn't, and all the stuff in between. The Oakland-based group Creative Interventions runs a Storytelling and Organizing Project (STOP), which collects narratives like these—instances in which violence was addressed or prevented without state intervention. These stories illustrate how people work every day, in their own ways, to change the circumstances and social structures that make it possible for violence to occur.

One STOP story recounts a situation in which a woman in Orange County, California, responded to domestic violence by seeking refuge at a friend's house. The friends then helped her reach out to other people to bring into her support network. The group listened closely to what the survivor wanted. Her mom assisted with getting her husband to leave her house (remaining calm despite his "raging") and convinced him to stay away, so the survivor could live there with her kids. Her network of family and friends then set up a schedule in which someone would come over every day and bring food and sit with her, and talk, if she was up for it. She explained, "It felt so good to have this full house, you know, this busy house of people coming by, and, you know, people were playing with the kids, and we were making art in the kitchen, and someone was always making tea, and it felt not alone." In the end, the survivor stressed that the community's response worked because she was able to say what she needed, and she was actively heard. She told STOP, "We need to trust people to be the experts on their own lives."[13]

In early January 2014, INCITE!, along with CURB and several other organizations, compiled a long list of transformative justice strategies for dealing with "police/vigilante/hate/white supremacist violence."[14] They emphasize that since approaches *need* to be community specific, they do not endorse any particular strategy. Instead, they're opening up a conversation about possibilities that will hopefully multiply, change, grow, and spread. Ideas include developing community centers that use transformative justice; gathering and circulating information about transformative practices used in other countries; starting up "neighborhood check-in" systems to keep connected with neighbors and ensure their safety (as opposed to vigilante-ish neighborhood watch groups); talking to people from hate groups directly (since they are, indeed, made up of individual people); using transformative justice strategies in workplaces; and many, many, many more.

"We Can't Do A Plus B Equals C"

INCITE!'s shared ideas demonstrate that "strategies" aren't always neatly sewn up, beginning-to-end stories that tidily close with the perpetrator held accountable and the survivor "sufficiently" healed. In fact, when I speak with Jenna Peters-Golden, a member of the Philly Stands Up! (PSU) collective that uses transformative practices to work with perpetrators of sexual assault, she tells me that she's not a huge fan of either numbers or anecdotes as metrics to measure success. "We can't do A plus B equals C here," Jenna tells me. "So we use small, specific tools." For example, she says, people who've caused sexual harm may tend toward narcissism; they're often better at focusing on themselves than noticing cues from others or engaging with others' feelings. So, Philly Stands Up! members stress considerate practices like showing up on time and asking, "How are you?" They're looking for shifts in behavior, changes in how people who've caused harm interact with those around them.

Jenna says, "When I'm meeting someone for a session, if they don't show up after twenty minutes, I'm not waiting—and if they call me later, I say, 'No, I'm not coming back; I'll see you next time. Showing up on time is a way of showing you respect me.'" Processes for working with perpetrators are lengthy, and Jenna tells me it may take a year before a person starts coming to meetings punctually and inquiring after other people's thoughts and emotions. "In the first twelve months, it's common for people to not remember to ask how my day has been, so I have to be pushy and say, 'I really want to tell you how I'm feeling,'" Jenna says. "Eventually, people start saying, 'How was your day?' They start listening."

In talking with people about transformative practices, Philly Stands Up! members emphasize that "eventually"; nurturing the possibility of lasting, evolving justice takes time. I ask scholar and activist Beth Richie, who's also a cofounder of INCITE!, how we then might begin to conceptualize a universe in which the widespread response to immediate violence—for example, the instant of an attack—is something other than *Call the cops*! "I think it is still an experiment, a way of thinking, and a call to develop something new," she says. "We need to take a long view." And that view isn't confined to the realm of harm response. New "ways of thinking" interweave with daily life, transforming our perceptions, our definitions, our experiences of justice, and our understandings of how to live together in the world.

Chapter 9

The Peace Room

When we think about the prison abolitionist movement ... it's not "Tear down all prison walls tomorrow," it's "crowd out prisons" with other things that work effectively and bring communities together rather than destroying them.

—*Andrea Smith, INCITE!: Women of Color Against Violence*[1]

As spring exhales its way into summer, I pay a visit to Manley High School in Chicago's North Lawndale neighborhood. In 2007, Manley logged the most "violent incidents" of any high school in the city—though of course such rankings will always be subjective, depending on which incidents are reported, which are dubbed violent, and who's counting.[2] Largely attended by black and Latino students, it's prime ground for the school-to-prison pipeline, in which school-based arrests pave a quick path to early incarceration. Research by Project NIA found that about one out of five juvenile arrests in Chicago in 2010 took place at a school. Seventy-five percent of those arrested were black youth, even though black kids make up only 42 percent of the Chicago school system.[3]

With racism entrenched in the punitive framework, that quick reach for the phone sets off a dismal chain—from the decision to call the police, to the police decision to arrest, to the decisions to charge, to convict, to incarcerate. Another common school punishment of choice, suspension, also fuels incarceration: When kids get stuck in a pattern of suspensions, they're much more likely to drop out of high school, and if they do, they're at least eight times more likely to be locked up than kids who graduate.[4] Plus, black students are more than three times more likely to be suspended than their white peers, according to the Office for Civil Rights.[5] In early 2014, the Obama administration acknowledged in letters to school districts that black students are disciplined more harshly.

A few years back, a student leadership development organization called Umoja set out to confront these issues by establishing a program that carves out a little corner of Manley High School, the "peace room," as a home base for restorative justice practices. The program revolves around a cluster of missions: to heal from and prevent violence, to forge positive community bonds, and to create a path for teachers, students, and administrators to respond to conflict in a community-based way, as opposed to triggering the sequence of suspension, arrest, juvenile detention, prison, torn-up families, and shattered lives. In many ways, the Umoja folks are struggling against the prison nation with every circle, every circumvented call to police. These are big goals for a small room.

When I arrive at the peace room, Umoja Program Director Ilana Zafran opens the door. Ilana's enthusiasm is immediately contagious—she is clearly in love with her job—and the aesthetic feel of the room also conveys an instant welcome. The walls here are plastered with brightly colored drawings, collages, huge glossy posters urging us to follow our dreams and embrace the world, to love ourselves and others. A big box in the corner overflows with sticks, balls, and trinkets—"talking pieces," which are used during circles to indicate who has the floor. A couple of girls are milling around, munching butter cookies; the space functions as a quiet hangout environment as well as a hub for addressing conflict.

When a fight has happened, or if one's brewing, the peace room kicks into high gear. In the program's early days, it was mostly security guards or teachers who would bring kids to the room for a circle. But as restorative justice has integrated into the fabric of the school's social environment, some kids have begun to view it as a natural intervention step when they see a situation going sour. Nowadays, friends of kids who've been harmed or done harm or threatened to hurt someone or talked about fighting may bring them down to the peace room—especially if those friends have experienced healing there themselves. Kids who've become entangled in violence or conflict sometimes take the initiative to come in themselves, as they come to better understand what "hurt" and "healing" feel like. As Fania Davis, founder of Restorative Justice for Oakland Youth puts it, just as hurt people hurt people, "healed people heal people."[6]

Ilana describes an incident that happened at Manley yesterday, in which two girls were about to fight but came to the peace room instead. "Earlier in the year, we would've seen them *after* they got in the fight," she says. Now they're still mad as hell at each other, but not fighting—and they've promised to come back and continue talking later today.

Before I had gotten here, I'd wondered, Why a room? Why not simply train teachers and kids in circles and other techniques, and let them give it a go in the classroom right away (which they're working to do now, along with the presence of the room)? When I ask, Ilana tells me that if you're practicing restorative justice in a conscious way, you can't assume that a cohesive community already exists. "It's about strengthening and building connections," she says, smiling at a kid wandering in from the hallway, his glasses askew. The peace room aims to be a safe community, woven into the fabric of the school, that is building toward a different type of system based around values of anti-violence and justice.

It strikes me as a stark contrast to in-school suspension rooms, where kids are often punished by near-abandonment in a classroom free of teaching and learning, left to drift toward boredom and frustration. In the 2010/11 academic year, the Chicago Public Schools handed 40,662 students out-of-school suspensions and 17,020 kids in-school suspensions.[7]

I turn to one of a cluster of girls munching cookies nearby—Gloria, she tells me loudly—and ask her why she comes to this room, even when she doesn't have to? She smiles and glances at a friend. "Well ..." she says, "this room pretty much kept me from getting in fights all the time. So that's a good thing!" The circles and informal chats that happen here helped her say her feelings out loud, to figure out why fights happen and what she can do to prevent them. "Yeah," says the friend. "Good because she was getting in fights with *me*! Then our friends started saying, '*Go to the peace room.*'"

Ilana jumps in, noting that not all conflicts resolve perfectly. "In some situations, the end resolution would be, I'm not gonna look at you, I'm not gonna talk to you, but we're not going to fight," she says. "It's about individual transformation, changing behaviors, learning more about what you're doing when you're making choices about how you treat people."

Gloria chimes in, "This room just safens things."

Crying over Spilled Milk

Before my idealized infatuation with the peace room can settle out to happy pasture, it becomes clear that this haven is not all laughter and sunny posters. A skinny sixteen-year-old boy plops down in the chair next to me and informs me, "Shit just got real."

It turns out that during a lunchroom food fight, a freshman boy, Dan,[*] threw a carton of milk at a junior, Johnny (the boy sitting beside me). According to Dan, Johnny proceeded to yell and curse at him, follow him to class, and make mocking faces at him from the doorway. A student teacher talked to them and they agreed to come to the peace room to hold a circle. (The question of what would have happened if they hadn't come—would they have gone to the security office, or the dean?—is a faint unknown hovering in the background.) The circle that will follow, Ilana explains to me, is not necessarily intended to "resolve the incident," but to diffuse the tension and make future conflict less likely.

Ilana's colleague, Kenny, takes Dan, a short, bewildered-looking kid who's staring at the floor, into another room for a preconference. He wants to know not only Dan's narrative of what happened just now, but also what happened before that—what kinds of interactions have Dan and Johnny had in the past? Do they have friends in common? And, of course, how is he feeling? Then Kenny comes back and Johnny's "preconference" begins:

Kenny: I'm here to get your side of the story.

Johnny: Well, I wanna hear his side.

Kenny: You do? That's great. Let's get your side first.

Johnny: You know, the lunchroom can be rowdy, and people are throwing things. I'm the type of person that, you know, I'm not gonna move just because people are throwing things. But I don't

---

[*] Names and inessential details have been changed to preserve the confidentiality of the circle.

throw things myself. It's childish. So, they're throwing milk and trays and apples and oranges and pizza, and fighting.... Then that little kid [Dan] come over and he starts throwing things. And then he threw milk! A whole milk at me! And it got all over the table, all over me. Ugh! I can't wash up here—I don't want to go around smelling like spoiled milk. So I just got outraged. Because I felt like it was disrespect. Like, you threw the milk at me to get me rowdied up. I'm lookin' around screaming, "Who did it, who did it??" My girl Lela started calming me down, and then some kid, that kid starts talking. He's saying, "Over milk?? You gonna get upset over milk?" We said some words. "Over milk?" I said, "Yeah, it's over milk, but how would you feel if I came and splattered milk all over the table and it got on you? You'd be doing the same thing. You might have even a worse reaction."

Kenny: You just said those words to him? You said them calmly?

J: Well no, I'm not gonna lie to you. I was yelling them at him. So then Lela calm me down. But then the boy come over there and he threaten to throw another milk at me! And that's when I really got outraged. But I didn't follow him. I'm not that type of person. But you know, I'm still not the type of dude that's gonna let you talk down to me. You gotta talk to me like I got some sense. And I talk to you that way. If he came up after and said, "Hey, I'm sorry about what happened," I'd say, "Fine."

K: So, it sounds like there's a couple pieces here. I'm just going to say it back to you and reframe a little, and you let me know if it sounds correct. It sounds like initially, a lot of things were going on, and you were already starting to feel a little frustrated at that point? When people were throwing things around?

J: Yeah, 'cause things was flying past my head!

K: So, do you have the sense that this boy purposely targeted you? Or could it have been actually an accident?

J: I think he purposely did it, because me and Lela sit there all the time and some people get jealous. You know, every time we hug … they think, oh I wish I had a relationship like that. You know, when we kiss, they say … oh, go get a room or something like that. So it could've been like that.

K: OK, so there could have been a reason. But could it have been a mistake?

J: OK, it could have been a mistake. But the way he handled it was just to go off at the mouth.

K: So, it was at that point really that you got upset.

J: Yeah.

K: But you were also upset when the milk first splashed you. So one question I have for you is, if you could hit pause at any point—you can't change anybody else, you can't change what happened—but if you could hit pause and *you* could have done something different, what would you have done differently?

J: Well, if they would've—

K: No, not them. You, you, you. [*They both laugh.*] What could you have done differently?

J: When I first saw the milk. Like if I hit pause, like one of them shows, I'd be like, "Click!"

K: Yeah, what would you have done?

J: I would've got up, picked up the milk, and threw it out. [*Laughter*]

J: No, but for real, I would've just got me and my girl out of the way.

K: So just move off to the side.

J: Yeah, and after that I would press play. And the milk would've hit the table. And nothing would happen. And no one would've got in a fight at all because ain't no one sitting there.

K: Which is a big difference from what you said at the beginning, which was, "I won't move for nobody." So here's the conflict then. You didn't move—because you felt like, I shouldn't have to move. They should go back to what they were doing. It was about the idea of disrespect. So—but you're saying now that maybe it wasn't worth it—that, looking back, if you knew that it was going to escalate how it did, that you would've had milk on you, that you might've almost gotten into a fight with a bunch of guys, you would've gotten out of the way first.

J: Right.

K: So it seems like maybe your actions, yelling out, "Who did it? Who did it?" didn't really get you what you wanted.

J: Yeah. I wanted to know who did it so I could confront them. See if it was a mistake. If it's a mistake, it's easier for me to let go. If you apologize, then OK.

K: So you wanted to know who did it. It wasn't just outrage? You were hoping to get an apology.

J: Right! That's it.

K: So do you see how maybe you getting up and shouting "WHO DID IT? WHO DID IT?" wouldn't make someone want to raise their hand and say, "Yes, it was me! I'm glad we have an opportunity to have this conversation." [*Laughter*]

K: So let's do a pause at that point, before you started yelling. What could you have done differently?

J: Well, if they would've—

K: No, not them. You, you, you. [*They both laugh.*] What could you have done differently?

J: I could have spoke calmly, calm and collected. Say, "Could someone please tell me who threw that milk, please?"

K: And explain why, right? Say, "Because …"

J: Because I feel disrespected! I feel disrespected, because how do I know you didn't do it on purpose?

K: So, to give yourself a little time to think about that, you could've maybe walked away at first and then … got to that point where you realized it wasn't worth it—that getting outraged wasn't the answer?

J: Yeah. I could just sit back?

K: Yes. Do you still feel like you need that apology?

J: You know—now I can let it go. It's over and done with.

K: That's great! So, that part is done with. But now we've got the other person, Dan—I'll bring him in here in a minute—but he feels like you didn't let things go, and now he's upset. He said you were going into his classroom afterwards. Did you go to that classroom? Did you know he was in that class?

J: I went there. I looked at him. I looked him dead in the eyes!

K: Yep, he said you went all the way into the classroom, looked at him, and left. So!

J: I didn't go in there for him, I went there because my girl's in there. But then I saw Dan in there, and he was getting up. I looked at him. I thought why's he getting up? In reality a freshman is not gonna whup a junior.

K: Can you see his perspective, that when you came in, it seemed like you were trying to keep things going?

J: He kept it going! He saw me in the hallways upstairs before class and he bumped me!

K: So, things are continuing to go on, whether we want to let it go or not. The other thing he's upset about is that he says you called him an "A." Do you remember calling him an "A"?

J: He said I called him an "A"? I probably did. I was outraged. I could've said anything.

K: So that's something you could admit to him. That you called him an A.

J: If I called him an A that's something I could admit. I could say, yeah, I called you an A! I remember! I said "stupid A." He threatened to throw another milk. I said, yeah, I want you to, you stupid A. I'll own up to it.

K: OK. I think that's one of the main things we want to do. To get to the point that you can own up to what you did. And we want to get you guys to the point where you're OK, and you can look at each other and say, hey, this is just about a little milk, right?

J: Don't cry over spilled milk! [*Laughter*]

K: Exactly! I'm so glad you said that. So it seems like you're at the point you could say to him, you know, I was upset when you threatened to throw another one …

J: Yeah.

K: So I'm gonna bring him in now. And so it's up to you whether you want to apologize or not.

J: Well, I apologize if I'm wrong. I want him to apologize for the milk, then I could apologize for calling him the name and the following. Hell, I could apologize first.

K: You can apologize? That's great!

J: Yeah, I can apologize.

K: All right, I'm going to talk quickly with Dan, and then I'll bring him in. I'll be right back.

[*Kenny goes away and returns with Dan and James, a student teacher who saw the fight.*]

K: All right, so things seemed to get out of control after something happened that seems relatively small, right? So we're coming together here to make sure we're done crying over spilled milk. Johnny?

J: Dan, I apologize for calling you that name. That was disrespectful towards you so I apologize for that.

[*James gives Johnny a high five.*]

K: I sense a lot of emotion right there! [*Laughter*]

James: That was a good move, man! That's very grown man!

K: Dan?

D: OK.

K: OK?

D: Me too. [*He pauses, with a frown.*] But why did he come to my class? What was that?

[*The bell rings; the school day has ended.*]

K: Dan, would you feel better if you had a little more time to think about this? We can pick back up tomorrow morning?

D: Yeah. I would.

K: All right! Let's pick this back up tomorrow. Think about all this tonight—and I'll see you at 8 a.m. tomorrow, here.

The kids wave vigorous goodbyes to Kenny, me, James, Ilana. The business of the peace room doesn't conclude when the bell rings. Dan's lingering concerns must be addressed; they will be prioritized over homeroom. If necessary, Umoja staff are available to meet with him alone—he can just stop by. That's why the room needs to be here every day, living inside the body of the school.

For most programs like Umoja, data on "success" is slim. How do you measure changed lifestyles, emotional transformations, strengthened friendships and family bonds? How do you measure the harm that *didn't* happen, that was prevented by circles like Johnny and Dan's? But a report from International Institute for Restorative Practices finds that six schools assessed throughout the country saw significant decreases in "disruptive behavior," reoffending, suspensions, expulsions, and violence after implementing restorative justice programs. [8] And in the Denver Public School system, implementing these types of practices yielded a 40 percent reduction in out-of-school suspensions and 68 percent reduction in the number of police tickets given in schools.[9]

For these programs to stand a chance, though, they need to be taken seriously and valued by everyone involved, including school administrators and other authority figures. They need to be *funded* and integrated into the school environment. Plus, as many schools become increasingly militarized, with metal detectors, police, and security patrolling the hallways, the presence of a peace room or even an infusion of community justice into the curriculum can't reverse that adversarial dynamic. One room devoted to peace can't topple a dominant culture based on control and punishment.

"There's a long way to go," Ilana tells me, walking me to the door as the kids file out toward the bus. "Ideally, there would be RJ and TJ people in every school—begin making it systematic.... A 'safe space' that's not just about a particular situation."

"Is Jail a Safe Space?"

"Safe space," a term that emerged out of the gay liberation and women's liberation movements,[10] is often used by groups practicing restorative and transformative justice. It's also a phrase that's sometimes been used to justify increased policing and state control to protect feelings of "safety" for certain (usually white, middle-class) groups over others.[11] The space envisioned by Umoja, though, is not a place you lock yourself inside. Rather, the kind of space that Ilana's talking about is open—it rejects isolation. It's a place, physical or not, where you can interact with your world and other humans freely, openly, and justly.

Susan Garcia Treischmann, the proprietor of Curt's Café, a community restaurant/training and support program for "at-risk" youth in Evanston, Illinois, talks about "safety" not as a cut-

and-dried objective reality that "nothing bad will ever happen to you," but as a feeling of freedom, understanding, and community engagement. She tells me that safety is partly about being cared for—and it's important for *everyone* to feel it, if it's going to work. In speaking of youth getting out of prison, Susan says, "You want to make the community feel safe and make the kid feel safe…. Oftentimes, what people don't realize is the offender is just as freaked out." When "the offender is freaked out," Susan continues, they're less likely to attempt to join with the community in positive ways, more likely to feel defensive, suspicious, and angry, and more likely to act on those feelings.

So, how can we, in the words of Gloria of Manley High School, "safen things"? How can we create an environment that doesn't just respond effectively to harm once it happens, but also fosters non-harm?

This is one of the largest questions in the universe, and one with which humans have been grappling since well before the rise of the prison-industrial complex. Much, obviously, has already been written about it. (Please check out the Resources section of this book for some great work by folks who have confronted the topic intensively!) However, I want to look at a few cases in which community is nurtured in creative ways, paving the road toward lasting, widespread, collective safety.

One such flashpoint is another incarnation of Umoja: Chicago's summer Community Builders (CB) program, which trains high school students—mostly poor students of color from neighborhoods with high rates of violence—in community-based justice principles and circle-keeping. In the summer of 2013, their focus is the concept of "safe space" itself: What defines it? What happens in its absence? How can we create it in our environments? At the end of the program, the kids go out into the community, initiating circles with different groups like park district summer camps and unemployment programs.

In the middle of summer in 2013, I walk over to the school where the CB kids will facilitate circles with groups of fifth-graders attending a summer program that meets at an elementary school in Evanston. The program aims to serve "young people whose needs are not being met by more traditional agencies"—mostly youth of color who come from impoverished backgrounds.

Shortly before the CB leaders, I enter the room where the first circle will convene. It's rowdy. One fifth-grader is industriously scooping dirt out of a flowerpot and depositing it on a table. Another kicks over a chair, screeching woefully, "She called me a *name!*" As they scramble into their seats, the circle keepers, four CB teens, write the "norms" (ground rules) in large letters on butcher paper taped to the wall. They explain that after someone in the circle has spoken, everyone will say "Ashe"—a Yoruba word often translated as "so be it," or "so it is." After a quick chat about the optimal definition of a "safe space"—open, positive, communicative, connection-driven, welcoming, no harm—the question is broached, "What's your safe space?" One of the teens discloses his (his basement, where he watches movies with his brothers and sister), and the kids simmer down, thinking. Ordinarily in a circle, the talking piece would be passed clockwise from person to person, but this circle's a little free-form. When a small child near the window frantically waves his hand, the talking piece, a stuffed dolphin, is tossed his way and he catches it. He says, "My safe space is my class at school, because I know everyone there!"

"Ashe!" we all sing.

"Getting to know your community," softly intones one of the teens, a tall girl of about seventeen. "That's a way of building safe space. Actually, we're doing it right now."

"Quiet places?" a pigtailed fifth-grader asks.

"Or places that are loud, because then you know there are other people around?" someone else wonders aloud, without requesting the talking piece.

Both receive nods and scattered "ashe"s; "safety" is subjective and situation dependent. Sometimes loud works, sometimes quiet works, sometimes it doesn't matter as long as you trust the people around you.

"OK!" says a tiny, smiling girl with huge glasses and a thin braid running down her back. "Then mine is my block, because the neighbors are friends, even the dogs and cats—if they come up to me, I'm not scared because I know them."

The frantic hand-waver chimes back in: "My block feels safe because I know a lot of the people—but the next block doesn't. The cops are always there."

I think of something Mariame Kaba said when I asked about fostering collective safety: "Get to know your neighbors—that's an investment." I think, also, of Todd Clear's research on how arrest and incarceration rips neighborhoods apart and, conversely, how community and connection-building can work to stem violence.

Then the smiling girl throws the talking piece to a short kid who cranes his head up to the circle-keeper standing next to him. He asks, "Is *jail* a safe space?"

Huh. Kayla has told me that for years she's seen prison as her only community, a place where she's formed bonds independent from heroin, despite institutional violence and oppression. I recall that fragment of a letter she sent me last summer: "Some of my best memories stem from inside these walls." And Jake Donaghy once wrote me about a friend of his who came back to prison on purpose: "'Freedom' was overwhelming and often dangerous. So she came back to what was familiar. What was predictable. Safe."

The Community Builder teens dart anxious glances at each other across the circle. Some of them have already been to juvenile detention. One offers, "No?" just as another says, "That's complicated, because you're not gonna get shot there. But we could talk about it later."

The first says, "Let's just say—you don't wanna go there. I know."

You're not gonna get shot there. The words hang in the air. In neighborhoods wracked by surveillance, racist policing, poverty, homelessness, and corresponding violence, is jail society's best offer of a means to "safety"—not just for the "public" outside, but for the people who are fed, clothed, housed, and not shot inside its walls, who are nevertheless subject to violence in countless other forms? In a prison nation, where "safety" so often means confinement of one kind or another, is the word even a useful focal point for building community?

A swarm of emotions engulfs the room, and no one says a thing for over a minute. Finally, a serious-looking, soft-spoken fifth-grade boy raises his hand for the talking piece. He catches it and looks around the circle, catching each person's eyes in turn. "I'm safe in my dreams," he says, "because there, you can't get hurt, even if you fall off a building or if somebody shoots you. And you don't have to be in jail. Just in your head. That's all."

The circle-keeper then calls on a tall, slumping girl, who shakes her head; she hasn't raised her hand. But then she shrugs and reaches for the talking piece. "He's right," she says. "I'm safe in my mind, because no one can take it away."

"Ashe," a small voice rises from a corner of the circle. "But I have a space to say, too."

It's a fifth-grade girl with huge eyes and a bow that might be bigger than her face perched atop her head. Someone rolls her the talking piece.

"I feel safe when I'm singing or dancing," she says. "When my whole family gets all together, and we can be singing and dancing, and that's something, you know? That's something safe."

As the Community Builders circle nears its end, the teens strike up a concluding activity that invokes that spirit of celebration: One of the teens sets a beat, tapping his foot and clapping, and the others join in, creating different beats with their hands and feet. Soon the kids join in, too. One kid pops in with a little tentative freestyling, which is met with lots of encouragement. As the beat dies down, the tiny smiling girl who mentioned her neighborhood dogs and cats gives the teen seated next to her a spontaneous hug.

The circle wraps up with a few big questions: "Was this circle 'safe'?" "How did that happen?" "What did we do to make it safe?" "How can you make spaces like this in your communities?"

The ideas these fifth-graders have brought forward represent a more sophisticated framework than many well-versed proponents of restorative justice proffer. The kids aren't talking about a fixed idea of "restoration." They're bringing up important contradictions and exposing assumptions about the concept of "safety," its uses and misuses. They are inquiring toward freedom, issuing, as Beth Richie put it, "a call to develop something new."

Of course, there needs to be relentless, ongoing discussion and action for a mentality of collective safety to develop—a safety that is for everybody. As Ilana says, it has got to be an organic part of the community. In fact, there needs to be a near-constant process of sticking-with-it if a movement for healing is going to mount a challenge to the existing criminal punishment template. But as that prescient seventeen-year-old noted, coming together—talking with each other—isn't just a precursor; it's an action, in and of itself.

As I exit the school, preparing to step out into the thick, damp heat, I think of what "community building" might have meant for my sister's teenage years. Kayla's downturn started when she began to get in trouble in school and was promptly discarded from our high school and sent to a higher-security school to be with the "bad kids." That school's goals were straightforward: enforcing the rules and getting the kids out as soon as possible, often not encouraging them to meet the requirements needed to enter college. Another of its goals: to root out the problem children from the regular high school, to promote "safety" for the "good kids." Soon after her transfer, Kayla tumbled into a spiraling sequence of probation, then juvenile detention, then a series of isolating rehabs, then jail, then prison. Who knows what would have happened if, at the slippery turning point, she'd been met with a welcoming community. Who knows—she might have found that physical place of peace, that place filled with familiar voices and just the right kind of silence. She might even have found a place of safety—or even better, freedom—in her mind.

"Where People Go Naturally": Peace Salons

Peace, of course, does not have to live in a room. A couple of months after my Umoja experience, I get in touch with Tasha Wilkerson, a youth services coordinator at a church in Chicago's Austin neighborhood, and a person who is intent on harvesting those peacemaking moments. Austin is a poor, predominantly black community on the city's West Side. It's home to the most-incarcerated block in the city.[12] As Tasha watched top-down violence "prevention" efforts in her community stop and start and stop again without making a dent, she grappled for a new framework, asking herself what moments of connection already thrived in this community and how they could be transformed into opportunities for making peace. What were the natural settings for "peace rooms" to materialize in Austin, and who would be the peacekeepers?

Tasha's answer: Hair salons, and the barbers who run them, often the recipients of their clients' stories of daily sadnesses, joys, conflicts, and connections. "I was thinking about the youth in the community and was considering where they go naturally, and who they trust to share what's really going on with them and in the street," she tells me. "I thought of salon owners because they are non-threatening, and youth go there for grooming on a regular basis on their own and accompanying their friends."

"Salons," in all their denotations, have always been places to which people gravitate to argue, discuss, and contemplate the big problems that rock the world and their own minds. They have ranged down the years from the Italian salons of the seventeenth century, in which well-to-do thinkers gathered at court to expound on philosophy and literature, to the vaguely rebellious French public salons that sort-of-welcomed commoners, to twentieth-century modernist gatherings geared toward imagining new genres of expression, to the African American–run beauty salons of the Jim Crow era that served as sites of economic independence and springboards for activism, to the contemporary salons that carry on that tradition, along with fostering conversations around gender, health, life struggles, culture, and relationships.

Dr. Tiffany Gill, author of *Beauty Shop Politics*, notes the historical importance of "how intentional beauticians were in using their space for political and health engagement and how these shops were linked to a national network. Women were often taught in beauty colleges how to engage their clients politically…. This was something that was very intentional, very thought-through, very much organized at the local, state and national level."[13]

Like the mid-century beauty school activists, Tasha set up a program at her church to train salon owners, this time in the art of the peace circle. The program's only been around a few months at the time of my interview, and, Tasha tells me, the salon owners haven't been convening formally structured circles. Instead, they've begun slipping in the new techniques in a more impromptu way, haircut by haircut, when a conversation veers toward issues of ongoing conflict or violence. "The owners of salons use the peacekeeping and circle-keeping skills in their regular day-to-day interactions with their clients," Tasha says. The idea is not to implement a standard response to problems, but to create an environment of honesty, understanding, and accountability where, ideally, the kernels of problems can be dealt with before they develop into deeper harm. In an interview with a local news network, Chicago organizer Cheryl Graves explains that the barber interventions are most useful for confronting interpersonal conflicts that might erupt into violence—disputes over girlfriends or boyfriends, or perceptions of disrespect.[14]

Peter Newman, who coordinates the Juvenile Justice & Child Protection Resource Section of the Chicago area's Circuit Court, has long urged the development of non-policing, alternative approaches to responding to harm. He is ecstatic about Tasha's efforts. He tells me, "We should be going to policymakers and saying, 'God, you're spending millions and millions of dollars on police and violence prevention—but look what just happened in Austin! They're supporting barbers and beauticians in doing this work.' This is how justice happens, when the structure is up to the individual communities. That's what's powerful."

Challenging the Idea of "Stranger"

What constitutes an "individual community"? Some of the most pernicious strains of violence are the forces that drive people from their homes, that inhibit even the idea of a permanent— or, at least, reliably existent—community. War does that. Settler colonialism does that. Gentrification does that. So does prison. Addressing that scattering and isolation has become a key focus of the Brooklyn-based Safe OUTside the System (SOS) collective (part of the Audre Lorde Project), which works to challenge violence that affects lesbian, gay, bisexual, trans, two-spirit, and gender-nonconforming people of color. SOS's Safe Neighborhood Campaign recruits places like religious institutions, schools, local businesses, and other public spots to become Safe Spaces, which agree to offer sanctuary to those fleeing violence and cultivate atmospheres of safety in daily life. The Safe Spaces have stickers in their windows so community members can identify them. Employees are educated about transphobia and homophobia and trained in addressing violence without calling the cops. Current Safe Spaces include bakeries, cafes, art galleries, a nightclub, and community organizing centers.

Alok Vaid-Menon, a collective member, tells me that especially in a rapidly gentrifying area like Central Brooklyn, it's crucial to "challenge the idea of 'stranger,'" to connect neighbors who might otherwise never meet due to the flux of people moving— or being forced—out and in. "The creation of Safe Spaces is … about bringing people together so that we can all see ourselves in community," Alok says. People who see each other, who realize they share a home, may well be more willing to intervene in a violent situation, more able to offer support to people facing violence, and better equipped to strengthen the community in ways that prevent violence in the first place.

Part of the process of creating safe space is transforming the conditions that pave the way for violence. Trans and gender-nonconforming people often face harassment, abuse, and violence in public restrooms, and are sometimes denied entry. Recently, SOS members worked with a Safe Space to provide gender-neutral bathrooms, aiming both to prevent the immediate violence that occurs in bathrooms and to foster a larger sense of collective safety for people of all genders.

As the Safe Neighborhood Campaign gains steam, members are hoping to take on other functions for which many people currently turn to police and prisons, such as investigating violent incidents and holding attackers accountable.[15] Alok says, "This is about making our communities recognize the power of resistance and safety that we already have!"

Growing Grace and Wisdom

Di Grennell is a Maori antiviolence activist living in northern New Zealand. Her town, Whangarei, and surrounding areas carry the weight of centuries of colonial violence—large-scale abuse that has traumatized residents and fueled domestic abuse in many families.

Di speaks of her brother-in-law, who, throughout his childhood, was regularly beaten at school for speaking his first language. In his adult life, despite his considerable wisdom and generosity, he often reacts to interpersonal problems with violence. One day, when his son threw a rock while playing and accidentally shattered the window of his father's car, the whole family knew the boy was in for a severe beating unless someone intervened. In an interview with the Oakland-based Storytelling & Organizing Project—part of the larger group Creative Interventions, mentioned in the previous chapter—Di describes how her relatives quickly mobilized to both shelter the boy and spur transformation:

> [The boy's] mother was on the phone to us right away. She was anxious to assure us that "that boy" would get it when his father came home.... So before he got home we burned up the phone lines—sister to sister, cousin to cousin, brother-in-law to sister-in-law, wife to husband, brother to brother. This was because my husband and his brother know that there are some lessons you are taught as a child that should not be passed on. The sound of calloused hand on tender flesh, the whimpers of watching sisters, the smell of your own fear, the taste of your own blood and sweat as you lie in the dust—useless, useless, better not born. This is a curriculum like no other. A set of lessons destined to repeat unless you are granted the grace of insight and choose to embrace new learning.
>
> So when the father of "that boy" came home and heard the story of the window, "that boy" was protected by our combined *aroha*, or love, and good humor, by the presence of a senior uncle, by invitations to decide how to get the window fixed in the shortest time for the least money. Once again phone calls were exchanged with an agreement being made on appropriate restitution....
>
> Next time my husband drove into the valley it was to pick up the car, and "that boy" was an anxious witness to his arrival. My husband also has very big hands, hands that belong to a man who has spent most of his life outdoors. These were the hands that reached out to "that boy" to hug, not hurt....
>
> This is only a small story that took place in an unknown valley, not marked on many maps. When these small stories are told and repeated so our lives join and connect, when we

choose to embrace new learning and use our "bigness" to heal not hurt, then we are growing grace and wisdom on the earth.

The building of peaceful spaces doesn't always need to stem from a formal program or predesigned initiative. The space Di's family created was situation-specific and spontaneous, forged in a matter of hours. It could happen because the neighbors knew each other—because of their "combined love."[16]

The world over, such spaces are being forged in both carefully sculpted and spur-of-the-moment ways. Of course, those two modes overlap: The family network that allowed Di Grennell to quickly mobilize a violence-prevention strategy was already in place, even though the exact plan to shield the boy from harm wasn't predetermined. As one of the Community Builders teens noted, the point of thinking about "safe space," ultimately, is to set about creating it where and when you can.

Harmful spaces are being built constantly and systematically, from military bases, to oil rigs, to juvenile detention centers, to "mental health jails," to police-targeted neighborhoods (Jazz's "open-air prisons"), to in-school suspension rooms, to prisons. Building spaces to counteract harm is a very different kind of project. These alternative spaces originate not from a preconstructed, one-size-fits-all, power-driven monolith, but from each of us. The "call to develop something new" isn't a mandate aimed only at lawmakers or community leaders, or at activists or intellectuals. It's a call that all of us must take up. Voices for Creative Nonviolence cofounder Kathy Kelly notes, "Some of this country's best minds are designing drones and weapons. We need them thinking about this instead!"

Chapter 10

A Wakeup

It's time to understand, go open-eyed into ourselves,
into our deepest fears, among our underground youth,
into the futureless future, and then rise up.
The time of sleeping is over.
　　　　　—Luis Rodriguez, "The Wanton Life"

Emerging from a childhood seared by poverty and gang violence, poet Luis Rodriguez was incarcerated briefly in 1970. Later, his son spent more than thirteen years in prison. In "The Wanton Life," Rodriguez writes of the prospect of a cultural awakening—not by way of brilliant innovation, but through the process of connecting, with both ourselves and those we have estranged, with eyes that remain open even as they drink in fear.

Incarceration may provide public reassurance that "dangerous" people have vanished and are therefore no longer in existence—but it also permits a different kind of closed-eyed comfort for those safely ensconced in non-prisonerhood. As Angela Davis notes, it veils homelessness. [1] (Lacino, running from foster care, living in stolen cars—locked up.) It veils poverty. (Sable, lawyerless, helpless to fight the contorted charges against her—locked up.) It veils illiteracy. (The 97 percent of prisoners who are assessed as not "proficient" in reading and writing—locked up.) It veils drug dependency. (Kayla, passed out on the street, homeless and near death, a needle in her arm—locked up.) And it veils racism—the criminalization of black and brown people, persisting over the centuries under the mask of "justice."

Maybe, then, part of confronting the destructive force of isolative punishment, of the mechanisms that grant power to the prison nation, is regaining sight. This means looking with open eyes at the suffering and oppression of "our underground youth." It means knowing that accountability isn't only an obligation thrust upon people when they've done harm. In order to end the "time of sleeping," we've all got to hold ourselves accountable to our community of humans.

"Everyday Abolition"

In a truly free world—a world freed of prison in its every incarnation—all structures related to "justice" would look different. The maintenance of "safety" wouldn't translate into brutal policing, surveillance, punishment, in-school suspension, imprisonment, isolation, chained birth, torn-up families, shattered communities.

But the fact that those structures still exist, and will likely continue to exist for generations as we work to transform them, doesn't mean that we can't resist perpetuating them ourselves. Chanelle Gallant, co-organizer of Everyday Abolition, a political art project focused on living prison abolition in daily existence, puts it like this: "I see abolition as something that isn't sort of a dreamy, lofty goal, that we need to wait for the revolution, but it's something that we actually need to create in our lives every day."[2]

In an email to me, Chanelle and her co-organizer Lisa Marie Alatorre list a few of the basics for enacting a world beyond imprisonment: universal education, mental and physical health care, housing, food, child care, trauma-informed therapy and healing programs, substance dependency treatment, recognition of treaty rights, and antiviolence and violence prevention programs, to name a few. The goal of abolition, Chanelle and Lisa tell me, is to "collectively approach life in a way that seeks safety, sustainability, and self-determination as necessary and possible for every single person."

Appropriately, the prison slang term for the day a prisoner is released is "a wakeup"—as in, when issuing a countdown, "twenty-nine days and a wakeup!" So what would a permanent wakeup look like?

Café Anti-Prison

Susan Garcia Treischmann's eyes are wide open. They have to be: She runs Curt's Café, a coffee shop in northwest Evanston, Illinois, that serves up delicious breakfasts and lunches, all the while functioning as a healing and training space for youth bound up in the criminal punishment system, many of whom are just emerging from prison. When I visit Susan at the restaurant around closing time, there are seventeen things going on at once, and she responds energetically to my interview questions while shifting furniture for an upcoming event, checking in on the kitchen, hollering instructions for tallying the day's revenue, and greeting kids who poke their heads in to say hi.

Susan comes to the movement from the high-end food service management world. "All I am is a restaurant person," she says humbly, though she's guiding hundreds of people in moving past their criminal records into healthier, more stable, more sustainable lives. Though Susan is trained in restorative justice, Curt's Café is a different kind of space from a circle or a peace room. The place is a sort of anti-prison, a microcosm of a society based on open eyes and human connectedness, on lifting that veil that allows us to ignore poverty, racism, homelessness, and illiteracy. Susan is responding to social problems with training, mentoring, and community linkages instead of surveillance and incarceration, striving toward the kind of world the Community Builders kids conjured up in their circle, a world in which people are active and feel whole and know their neighbors.

At Curt's, "at-risk" youth—people aged fifteen to twenty-two who've been caught up in the system or seem to be headed that way, many of whom are poor youth of color—can come to learn both job skills and life skills, becoming part of a community that both cares for them and holds them accountable. (Susan doesn't hesitate to chew them out if they slack.) They receive a stipend, and if they stick with it they may well be hired on staff.

Plenty of rehab centers have businesses attached, but Curt's is not a "jobs program." Joining the café community is intended to be transformational: Youth come in having gotten stuck on one or more "wrong paths," and, ideally, come out heading in new, healthier, safer directions. When they start meandering down harmful roads again, they're not punished or banished. Instead, they're held accountable.

It's not simple, by any contortion of the imagination.

"The first month, they don't show up," Susan says. "Last week, I had three kids come in very late because they were out partying the night before. So rather than firing them I sat them down and I'm like, 'All right, so who was affected by this?' They say, 'Nobody!' Then we went through the ripple effect. Three people walked out because I couldn't get them coffee. People called on the phone and didn't get an answer. And how about the next group of kids that want to come into the program? If those kids think we're a bunch of losers, they're not going to come in."

Usually, she says, the kids start showing up—they don't want to let their community down.

Meanwhile, volunteers are paired with each youth, and mentors and counselors are on hand. Curt's has literacy tutors, math tutors, GED tutors. Formerly incarcerated youth are taught how to open a bank account. Mentors can help kids living in extreme poverty procure the basics, like medical care. Instead of sending people to a jumble of different support programs for job skills, life skills, and counseling, they get it all at Curt's, in ways that are naturally linked, Susan explains:

> We wash dishes with them and we talk about, "What'd you do last night?" or, "Wouldn't there be a consequence to beating that guy up? If you end up back in jail then *he* actually wins that fight, right?" They don't have to look at us, we're all at the sink. When we're doing barista training and teaching them how to make espressos, we're really talking about, "Do your parents drink coffee at home? Oh, your dad just left home. That must be hard.…"

I think of how advocates of restorative and transformative justice talk about how those practices need to be ways of life, not just responses to harm. Curt's is an effort to cultivate that way of life while maintaining an awareness that kids are getting tripped up in the system for all kinds of reasons—that through pipelines of racism, poverty, and fractured communities, they're tumbling toward a "futureless future." The café is building an alternate way forward, not only by teaching skills and creating community, but by modeling the kind of society we *could* be.

"Hand-holding"

On the Everyday Abolition blog, performer and activist Micha Cárdenas writes that isolation can be a type of violence: "Sometimes violence looks like being disconnected from community, lacking a community structure of support, struggling alone, reaching out for help, trying to get somewhere safer, or watching others struggle and not feeling able to help."[3]

Susan stresses the importance of "hand-holding" for people who are alone and struggling. "Hand-holding" has a negative connotation, akin to coddling. But holding hands is one of the most basic human gestures of connection. It calms anxious neurons, easing stress and diminishing that so-often-unhelpful emotion, fear.[4] It conveys both closeness and vulnerability—if you're using your hand to "hold," you're not using it to fight.

I ask Susan if she thinks that this metaphorical "hand-holding" could actually propel us toward a different approach to social problems, transforming prison-nation tactics of supposed harm prevention. She says yes: "If we were to make our system really about that, we would end the cycle. All that's stopping us is ourselves."

Of course, though Curt's Café functions as a transformational community, it still exists within the clutches of a prison society. Right now, four of the program's kids are homeless. "That's a really hard thing for us to come at," Susan says, adding that untreated drug and alcohol dependency are other common issues that often interfere with progress. Of the homeless youth, Susan says, "They can't be here and feel safe. They're falling asleep all the time, they're not eating well. We've got one kid, we were able to get him to a dentist—his wisdom teeth are growing in badly. A volunteer is willing to pay to have them removed because he's in so much pain. But where's he gonna recupe? On a park bench?

Didn't think about that end of the problem! So we're learning as we go."

#InsteadofPrisons

The question of the homeless wisdom tooth patient raises an inevitable quandary: Even as we struggle to cultivate more just systems of living together in the world, we're inevitably also still living inside the prison nation. The wisdom tooth is fixed, but the structures that keep this kid and millions of others in destitute poverty and bound up in the criminal punishment system cannot be "solved" through the gift of that surgery. Places like Curt's set a transformational example: cultivating a new community, one filled with support, education, delicious food, and possibilities for the future. But how can we bring Curt's to the world? As the prison walls crumble, how do we concretely redirect the energy that has gone into powering prisons and funnel it into the things we need to grow a sustainably connected, just, safe, interesting, fun, pro-humanity society?

In November 2012, members of the group Decarcerate PA assembled a large model of a "little red schoolhouse" (complete with a chimney) and a row of school desks (complete with note-books and apples) on the grounds of a construction site where the building of two new prisons had commenced. Then they sat at the desks and linked arms, chanting, "Tear down the jail-house, build up the schoolhouse." When seven of them were arrested over an hour later, prison construction vehicles were forced to literally tear down the model schoolhouse and clear out the desks, notebooks, and even apples, in order to enter the site and resume building. The action, carried out "alongside a public tribunal where prisoner family members and formerly incarcer-ated people provided testimony in support of moratorium on prisons," may have been the first-ever nonviolent sit-in to block prison construction.[5]

Decarcerate PA is not focused *only* on halting prison expansion and reducing populations; members are also envisioning what a post-prison world would look like and live like. They draw a firm connection between increased prison funding and decreased education funding (Philadelphia has recently closed dozens of schools in poor, mostly black neighborhoods), and the need to reverse those trends. Member Layne Mullett emphasizes that the group rejects any talk of students being more important than prisoners and thus more deserving of funding; the goal is to get people out and shrink the budget, freeing up more money for education and other priorities that build community.

Decarcerate PA partners with teachers' unions, student groups, labor groups, civil liberties groups, and immigrant rights groups. Incarcerated people and their loved ones form an integral part of the coalition. "We must understand we're part of a larger movement," Hakim Ali, a founding member of the organization, tells me over the phone.

In late spring 2013, Decarcerate PA organized a 113-mile march from Philadelphia to the state capital of Harrisburg, where they arrived just in time to hold a rally aimed at legislators returning to debate the annual budget. Along the way, members stopped off in towns large and small, holding community discussions and asking residents to make flags illustrating their answers to the question, "What would you build instead of prisons?" They posed the question to people in prisons, jails, and detention centers, too. Then they blasted the answers all over the Internet, creating a "100 Days of 'Instead of Prisons'" brainstorm marathon, posting a flag photo on their website each day and using the hashtag #insteadofprisons to generate discussion via social media.

Most of the ideas are founded on principles of coming together: "Libraries!" "Youth orchestras!" "Healthy lunches, books, arts programs!" "Fully funded birth centers!" "Internet access!" "Mental health care!" "Swimming pools in every neighborhood!" And vitally: "Family dinners with *no one* at the table missing!"

SOS

Reginald Akkeem Berry, one of the formerly incarcerated activists who led the charge to close down Tamms, knows something about missing family dinners, having spent seventeen years behind bars—eight of them in the supermax prison where, every night, he ate alone. But, he says, his wife and sons stuck with him over the years, visiting and calling when permitted, writing when not. "As one year turned to five, five to ten, ten to fifteen, they helped me remain focused until I was emancipated," Akkeem tells me over the phone. Akkeem is a former gang leader (ex-chief of the Four Corner Hustlers), and during much of his time behind bars he continued to occupy a position of authority in the gang. It was his sons, he says, who inspired him to break ties with the gang and shift to anti-violence organizing, not only with the Tamms campaign, but also within his own neighborhood. The motivation came to him in sleep, midway through his time in prison.

"I had a dream of a ship being tossed to and fro in the water, with someone standing at the edge, holding up a sign. It said 'SOS,'" he says. "I woke up in a sweat. I interpreted this as my sons, my sons and the kids in my community—those kids were in turbulent waters. They needed help."

That energy carried Akkeem forward when he was released, and he went on to create an "SOS" of his own: an organization called Saving Our Sons Ministries, geared toward helping youth avoid violence and creating opportunities for jobs, mentorship, sports, arts, and a five-week summer enrichment program called Keep Kids Learning. He and his wife "adopted" Delano Elementary School, which they had both attended themselves. They cultivated programs to "change the school's mentality," including a playground renewal project, clothing and school supplies giveaways, and a yearly peace rally. Just having more adults maintain a visible presence in the school area makes violence less likely, Akkeem notes.

His observation circles back to that transformative logic: Connection and community accountability—*not* prison and policing—are the routes to a safe, just, compassionate, free society. Akkeem critiques the "Safe Passage" program, a city-sponsored, police-led program with a similar aim that stations adult monitors, subject to a rigorous criminal background check, along school routes. In theory, he says, it's a great idea—but the adults involved aren't actually people from the community. "You could send a Harvard PhD out on that corner, who never had a [criminal] case [against him], and let him try to tell the guys to keep it moving," Berry told DNAInfo Chicago last year. "What's gonna happen? They're gonna run him off that corner."[6]

Meanwhile, Akkeem leads actions to call out lawmakers for the way they've abandoned communities of color. He's spoken out against Chicago's school closings (most of which took place on the West and South Sides) and continues to condemn the state's prison budget. He heads up rallies and press conferences, pointing to issues like the lack of jobs available to black men on Chicago's West Side. "Every day, we need to invest in the community we live in," he says.

For a long time, "investing in our community" has served as a justification for policing, surveillance, arrests, monitoring, incarceration, and discrimination, in the name of "safety." And so building the kinds of communities that break free of those institutions requires not only concrete action, but also a continual remaking of the perceptions and motivations that guide our interactions—with the people across the street, the people we work with, the people we pass in the grocery store, the people we live with, the people we love. Chanelle and Lisa from Everyday Abolition explain, "It is about pulling the cops out of our hearts and minds and radically rethinking safety and justice."

Health Without Cages

One of the many priorities that Chanelle and Lisa point to as an abolitionist goal is free treatment for those who suffer from substance dependency, an issue that's frequently bound up with incarceration, as my family well knows. Mandatory "rehabilitation" (akin to the "mental health jails" of which CURB warns) is sometimes proffered as an alternative to incarceration. But really effective treatment means bringing people *out* of isolation—not imposing more of it.

Comprehensive, widely accessible, family- and community-oriented, optional treatment should be cost-free and available for all those who want to commit to addiction recovery. For those who don't choose to make that commitment, accessible and condition-sensitive medical care must still be provided: You can't force a person to recover, but that doesn't mean abandoning them to a "futureless future." Precedents for this kind of medical care exist elsewhere in the world. For example, in Canada, Switzerland, Australia, Germany, Spain, and Norway, legal safe injection centers provide heroin users with a place to administer their drugs safely, with medics looking on to assist with overdose prevention, administer emergency care, and deliver information about safer usage practices. Clean needles are provided, and the medical team offers other services for folks who typically avoid official health institutions (and other institutions) whenever possible. Plus, there's plenty of info and guidance on treatment for those who are interested.

Results—those you can document, since life satisfaction, ability to participate in one's family and community, and personal fulfillment can't really be measured—are reliably good. In the Swiss program, the on-the-spot medical treatment has ensured that no one has died from an overdose. And upon discharge, about half of participants ended up enrolling in recovery-oriented treatment programs. A British study demonstrated that participants, who were provided with counseling and social services in addition to heroin administration, got healthier and happier, and many were able to find housing and jobs. As a bonus, "the number of crimes committed by those in the group dropped from 1,700 in the 30 days before the program began to 547 in the first six months of the trial." And another plus: By the end of the trial, three-quarters of the study group had stopped using street heroin.[7] These programs aren't perfect, but in an imperfect world they're crucial public health measures that save lives. And survival is a key component of freeing ourselves from the logic of prison. If no one is disposable, then everyone must be granted the necessities and the tools that enable them to live.

Liberation

The monumental shift toward a system structured by connection instead of isolation will be a shift so deep that it will leave this country unrecognizable. Just as much as it is a transformation of systems, it is a transformation of priorities, of how we define a good society and a good life. Angela Davis argues that prison abolition is necessarily a movement for a wholly different world, "a world that doesn't *need* to depend on prisons," because people's needs are met in other—life-giving, life-affirming—ways.[8]

As I'm wrapping up my conversation with Jazz Hayden from Campaign to End the New Jim Crow, he adds one last crucial point. We've got to work toward specific changes every single day, he says, but we also have to start telling ourselves different stories. "As long as we continue using the narrative of the few when we talk about the many, we're walking through the poppy fields, falling asleep, like in *The Wizard of Oz*," he says. "We have to tell the truth, and act on the truth. This is our planet, and as far as we know, this is the only planet in the cosmos we can live on. It's for all of us. We have to wake up."

The struggle to end the prison nation is not an isolated fight. It's a culture-wide leap toward liberation from all manifestations of imprisonment—a liberation that can only arise through coming together.

"Human lives are what weighs in the balance," Lacino Hamilton writes to me, as fall begins to turn to winter. "What are we waiting for?"

Epilogue

Not an Ending

"Two days and a wakeup!" Kayla howls ecstatically into my ear during a November phone call from prison. "My babyyy! I'm gonna see my baby in *two days*!"

"You did it!" I say.

"Yeah," Kayla sighs. She pauses for so long I think she has hung up, and a sudden nausea descends—I'm worried she's about to announce that she'll miss prison.

Instead, she says, "Don't worry, My. This time I *know* it's going to be hard."

The sequence of these two thoughts—the reunion with Angelica, the recognition that release doesn't erase the reality of incarceration—reminds me that mixed with most released prisoners' joy is the knowledge that they're actually transitioning to a different facet of the prison-industrial complex. Parole is a subtler but still very present confinement. Kayla must not only stay clean but also conform to other conditions (curfew, treatment sessions, location restrictions) if she is to steer clear of reincarceration. And although the Department of Child and Family Services has thankfully granted Kayla custody of her own child (at first, they had threatened to deny her that), they will be conducting ongoing surveillance of her parenting.

Still, this time, upon release, some things are different. Kayla is taking a big step of her own accord, *not* dictated by mandates or monitoring. She has opted to enter the recovery home at Women's Treatment Center (WTC), a publicly and donation-funded program that offers previously incarcerated mothers a chance to recover from drug problems in a safe, supportive environment, *with* their babies. It's one of the only centers of its kind in the state.

The program is controversial: It doesn't fit too comfortably into the prison-nation mindset. In a newsletter, WTC's director writes, "I've had a prospective funder tell me, 'We don't fund drug addicts and criminals.'"[1] Though some women are able to opt for the center as an alternative to incarceration, others choose to enter it completely of their own accord, and can do so cost-free. The "home" area, where Kayla is staying, is a place where, instead of being "caught" and disciplined through treatment, women can turn voluntarily because they want to break with their dependencies and nurture new lives. WTC also provides the basics: food and reasonably comfortable shelter.

These women are not punished with isolation and separation from their kids for things like addiction, poverty, and single motherhood. Instead, they are given the support to nurture bonds, develop friendships, and care for their children, and are provided with assistance for procuring subsidized housing in the future. Although the women completing "alternative sentences" are confined in their movement (unfortunately, the treatment center can't simply negate the criminal punishment system), many others have the freedom to leave, get a job, attend meetings, see family, go to the gym, go to a movie—to connect.

After a couple of months with her baby at the recovery home, Kayla tells me over the phone, "I'm just watching her sleep, and I'm the happiest I've ever been in my life." While she was in prison, she began compiling a journal for Angie (as she now calls Angelica), filled with pictures, letters, and poems. She shows me a poem she's written about her gratitude for the reunion. A fragment of it:

She won't grow up w/o a mother
Or call another person mom
Such a fragile existence seems destined to fail but
That little girl is my world
It's up to me to shelter her from the one I brought her into
The same one I've been trying to escape instead of taking
The time to embrace...
It's time to learn

As my phone conversation with Kayla draws to a close, I'm unspeakably grateful that it's ending on our own terms, not because our allotted time is over, or because my prepaid account has run out, or because an officer has ordered a lockdown. I'm grateful that next time I want to hear Kayla's voice, I can pick up the phone and call her myself—and hey, we can even hug each other without a barked order to stay within a foot of a visiting room table! More than all that, I'm thankful that she and Angie are together—that they're not split by handcuffs, shackles, or the watchful eyes of a guard, and not counting down the minutes until they'll be severed from each other's arms.

The poem is also a sobering reminder of all the mothers still wholly engulfed in the system. For so many women, the first line of Kayla's poem will never ring true. Kayla is incredibly fortunate that, with the support of both a family with whom she's still connected and the new community she's building at the recovery home, she has a lot of accompaniment in meeting those benchmarks. She says that, for the first time in as long as she can remember, she's "free."

I don't know where things will stand a month from now, so I can't call this a happy ending. It's simply not an *ending*, and it never will be. But for Kayla, the "sun has come" for the first time in many years. What's sustaining her now, she tells me, is love—a force that's antithetical to imprisonment, a force that regenerates connective tissue and breathes life into dead links, when it's free to flourish.

Permitted to be with her child and supported in that endeavor, permitted to reunite with her family, she tells me that she is alive again. She is able to think about the future with a sense of hope—one of the greatest freedoms of all.

"I'm going to make wasted nights, sick mornings, a trapped mind and locked away body all things of the past," Kayla writes, in another poem. "Life is amazing. I want to be part of it."

Notes

Introduction: Into the Hole

1 Angela Y. Davis, "Masked Racism: Reflections on the Prison-Industrial Complex," *ColorLines* (Fall 1998). Retrieved from www.thirdworldtraveler.com/Prison_System/Masked_Racism_ADavis.html.

2 Lucy McKeon, "When Violence Backfires," *Salon*, June 2, 2012. Retrieved from www.salon.com/2012/06/02/when_anti_violence_backfires/.

3 Pew Center on the States, *State of Recidivism: The Revolving Door of America's Prisons* (Washington, D.C.: Pew Center on the States, 2011. Retrieved from www.michigan.gov/documents/corrections/Pew_Report_State_of_Recidivism_350337_7.pdf.

Chapter 1 The Visiting Room

1 John Tierney, "Mandatory Prison Sentences Face Growing Skepticism," *New York Times*, December 11, 2012.

2 Lauren E. Glaze and Laura M. Maruschak, "Parents in Prison and Their Minor Children." Bureau of Justice Statistics, US Department of Justice, 2008. Retrieved from http://bjs.gov/index.cfm?ty=pbdetail&iid=823.

3 Jeremy Travis, "Summoning the Superheroes: Harnessing Science and Passion to Create a More Effective and Humane Response to Crime," in *To Build a Better Criminal Justice System: 25 Experts Envision the Next 25 Years of Reform*, edited by Marc Mauer and Kate Epstein (Washington, D.C.: Sentencing Project, 2012), 12.

4 Bruce Drake, "Incarceration Gap Between Whites and Blacks Widens." Pew Research Center, 2013; www.pewresearch.org/fact-tank/2013/09/06/incarceration-gap-between-whites-and-blacks-widens/.

5 Sarah Schirmer, Ashley Nellis, and Marc Mauer, *Incarcerated Parents and Their Children: Trends 1991–2007* (Washington, D.C.: Sentencing Project, 2009). Retrieved from www.sentencingproject.org/doc/publications/publications/inc_incarceratedparents.pdf.

203

6 Randall G. Sheldon and Selena Teji, "Collateral Consequences of Interstate Transfers of Prisoners," Center on Juvenile and Criminal Justice, 2012. Retrieved from http://www.cjcj.org/uploads/cjcj/documents/Out_of_state_transfers.pdf.

7 Ram A. Cnaan, Jeffrey Draine, Beverly Frazier, and Jill W. Sinha, "Ex-Prisoners' Re-Entry: An Emerging Frontier and a Social Work Challenge," *Journal of Policy Practice* 7, nos. 2–3 (2008): 178–98.

8 "Prisoners and Families Connect with Video Visitation, for a Price," *Prison Legal News*, September 9, 2012.

9 Sadhbh Walshe, "Prison Video Visits Threaten to Put Profit Before Public Safety," *Guardian*, October 25, 2012.

10 "Attica Correctional Facility," Correctional Association of New York, www.correctionalassociation.org/wp-content/uploads/2012/05/Attica_3-17-05.pdf.

11 Creasie Finney Hairston, "Prisons and Families: Parenting Issues During Incarceration," report of the project From Prison to Home: The Effect of Incarceration and Reentry on Children, Families, and Communities, U.S. Department of Health and Human Services/Urban Institute, 2001. Retrieved from http://aspe.hhs.gov/hsp/prison2home02/hairston.htm.

12 Grant Duwe and Valerie Clark, "Blessed Be the Social Tie That Binds: The Effects of Prison Visitation on Offender Recidivism," *Criminal Justice Policy Review*, December 6, 2011.

13 "About the Federal Bureau of Prisons," Federal Bureau of Prisons, US Department of Justice, January 2011. Retrieved from www.bop.gov/news/PDFs/ipaabout.pdf.

14 R. Cross, "A Prison's Family Plan," *Chicago Tribune*, October 2, 1985.

15 Christopher Hensley, ed., *Prison Sex: Policy and Practice* (Boulder, Colo.: Lynne Reinner Publishers, 2002), 144.

16 Ibid., 149.

17 *Lyons v. Gilligan*, 382 F. Supp. 198 (1972).

Chapter 2 The 100-Year Communication Rewind

1 Elizabeth Greenberg, Eric Dunleavy, and Mark Kutner, *Literacy Behind Bars: Results from the 2003 National Assessment of Adult Literacy Prison Survey*, Report NCES 2007-473 (Washington, D.C.: National Center for Education Statistics, US Department of Education, 2007).

2 Detroit Regional Workforce Fund, *Addressing Detroit's Basic Skills Crisis*, August 2012. Retrieved from http://readingworksdetroit.org/basicskills.pdf.

3 National Center for Education Statistics, *A First Look at the Literacy of America's Adults in the 21st Century* (Washington, D.C.: National Center for Education Statistics, US Department of Education, 2005).

4 Schirmer, Nellis, and Mauer, *Incarcerated Parents and Their Children*, 2.

5 Reporters Committee for Freedom of the Press, *The First Amendment Handbook*, 2011. Retrieved from www.rcfp.org/first-amendment-handbook/8-access-places/introduction-journalists-right-access-access-prisons-and-pr.

6 Texas Civil Rights Project, *Banned Books in the Texas Prison System: How the Texas Department of Criminal Justice Censors Books Sent to Prisoners* (Austin: Texas Civil Rights Project, 2011). Retrieved from www.texascivilrightsproject.org/docs/prisonbooks/TCRP_Prison_Books_Report.pdf.

7 John Dannenberg and Alex Friedmann, "FCC Order Heralds Hope for Reform of

Prison Phone Industry," *Prison Legal News*, December 2013.

8 Whet Moser, "The Cost of Phone Calls in Cook County Jail to Drop," *Chicago Magazine*, December 4, 2012.

9 Brandon Sample, "Increasing Number of Prisoners Obtain Access to Email," *Prison Legal News*, December 2009.

Chapter 3 On the Homefront

1 Marion Scher, "Stigma: The Mark of Shame," *South African Psychiatry Review* 9, no. 2 (May 2006), www.cartercenter.org/news/documents/doc2389.html.

2 Jeremy Travis, Elizabeth Cincotta McBride, and Amy L. Solomon, *Families Left Behind: The Hidden Costs of Incarceration and Reentry* (Washington, D.C.: Urban Institute Justice Policy Center, 2005).

3 Danielle H. Dallaire, "Incarcerated Mothers and Fathers: A Comparison of Risks for Children and Families," *Family Relations* 56, no. 5 (December 2007): 440–53.

4 *Reauthorization of Three Programs: The Mentoring of Children of Prisoners Program, the Promoting Safe and Stable Families Program, and the Court Improvement Program, Before the House Committee on Finance*, 109th Cong. (2006) (testimony of Joan E. Ohl).

5 Ernest Drucker, *A Plague of Prisons: The Epidemiology of Mass Incarceration in America* (New York: New Press, 2013), 160.

6 Susan D. Phillips, Wendy Cervantes, Yali Lincroft, Alan J. Dettlaff, and Lara Bruce, eds., *Children in Harm's Way: Criminal Justice, Immigration Enforcement, and Child Welfare* (Washington, D.C.: Sentencing Project/First Focus, 2013).

7 Michelle Alexander, *The New Jim Crow: Mass Incarceration in the Age of Colorblindness* (New York: New Press, 2010).

8 Dina R. Rose, Todd R. Clear, and Judith A. Ryder, *Drugs, Incarceration and Neighborhood Life: The Impact of Reintegrating Offenders into the Community* (Washington, D.C.: US Department of Justice, 2002).

9 Ibid.

10 Todd R. Clear, Dina R. Rose, Elin Waring, and Kristen Scully, "Coercive Mobility and Crime: A Preliminary Examination of Concentrated Incarceration and Social Disorganization," *Justice Quarterly* 20, no. 1 (March 2003): 33–64.

11 Ibid.

12 Ibid.

13 Dorothy E. Roberts, "The Social and Moral Cost of Mass Incarceration in African American Communities," *Stanford Law Review* 56, no. 5 (April 2004): 1288.

14 Todd R. Clear, *Imprisoning Communities: How Mass Incarceration Makes Disadvantaged Neighborhoods Worse* (New York: Oxford University Press, 2007).

15 Beth Richie, *Arrested Justice: Black Women, Violence, and America's Prison Nation* (New York: New York University Press, 2012), 99–100.

16 Patricia Tjaden and Nancy Thoennes, *Extent, Nature and Consequences of Intimate Partner Violence: Findings from the National Violence Against Women Survey* (Washington, D.C.: National Institute of Justice, US Department of Justice, and the Centers of Disease Control and Prevention, 2000).

17 Richie, *Arrested Justice*, 119.

Chapter 4 "Only Her First Bid"

1 New York State Department of Corrections and Community Supervision, *Parolee Facts*, 2011. Retrieved from www.parole.ny.gov/program_stats.html.

2 Pew Center on the States, *State of Recidivism: The Revolving Door of America's Prisons* (Washington, D.C.: Pew Center on the States, 2013).

3 Matthew R. Durose, Alexia D. Cooper, and Howard N. Snyder, *Recidivism of Prisoners Released in 30 States in 2005: Patterns from 2005 to 2010* (Washington, D.C.: Bureau of Justice Statistics, US Department of Justice, 2014).

4 Judith Greene and Néstor Ríos, *Reducing Recidivism: A Review of Effective State Initiatives* (Brooklyn, N.Y.: Justice Strategies, 2009).

5 Pew Center, *State of Recidivism*.

6 John Tierney, "For Lesser Crimes, Rethinking Life Behind Bars," *New York Times*, December 11, 2012

7 Pew Charitable Trusts, "States Cut Both Crime and Imprisonment," December 2013. Retrieved from www.pewstates.org/research/data-visualizations/states-cut-both-crime-and-imprisonment-85899528171.

8 National Advisory Commission on Criminal Justice Standards and Goals, *A National Strategy to Reduce Crime: Final Report* (Washington, D.C.: Government Printing Office, 1973), 358 and 597.

9 Rose, Clear, and Ryder, *Drugs, Incarceration and Neighborhood Life.*

10 Christie Thompson, "Are California Prisons Punishing Inmates Based on Race?" *Propublica*, April 12, 2013.

11 *Hovater v. Robinson*, 1 F.3d 1063, 1068 (10th Cir. 1993) (stating that "an inmate has a constitutional right to be secure in her bodily integrity and free from attack by prison guards" (citing *Alberti v. Klevenhagan*, 790 F.2d 1220, 1224 (5th Cir. 1986))).

12 Cindy Struckman-Johnson and David Struckman-Johnson, "A Comparison of Sexual Coercion Experiences Reported by Men and Women in Prison," *Journal of Interpersonal Violence* 21 (December 2006): 1591–615.

13 Just Detention International, "LGBTQ Detainees Chief Targets for Sexual Abuse in Detention," 2009. Retrieved from: www.justdetention.org/en/factsheets/JD_Fact_Sheet_LGBTQ_vD.pdf; D. Morgan Bassichis and Dean Spade, *"It's War in Here": A Report on the Treatment of Transgender and Intersex Prisoners in New York State Men's Prisons* (New York: Silvia Rivera Law Project, 2007). Retrieved from http://srlp.org/files/warinhere.pdf.

14 Bassichis and Spade, *It's War in Here.*

15 L. Griffith, *The Fall of the Prison: Biblical Perspectives on Prison Abolition* (Grand Rapids, Mich.: Erdmans, 1993), 106.

16 Catherine Hanssens, Aisha C. Moodie-Mills, Andrea J. Ritchie, Dean Spade, and Urvashi Vaid, *A Roadmap for Change: Federal Policy Recommendations for Addressing the Criminalization of LGBT People and People Living with HIV* (New York: Center for Gender & Sexuality Law at Columbia Law School, 2014).

17 Drucker, *A Plague of Prisons*, 131.

18 Richard Shelton, *Crossing the Yard: Thirty Years as a Prison Volunteer* (Tucson: University of Arizona Press, 2007), 51.

19 Urban Institute, "Family Support Is Key to Staying Out of Prison, Say Ex-Offenders in Chicago," 2004. Retrieved from www.urban.org/publications/900762.html.

20 For more on this issue, see Melissa Gira Grant's 2014 book, *Playing the Whore: The Work of Sex Work* (New York: Verso/Jacobin, 2014).

21 Sonja B. Starr and M. Marit Rehavi, "Mandatory Sentencing and Racial Disparity," *Yale Law Journal* 123, no. 1 (October 2013): 39.

22 Jonathan Vankin, "Bank Robber Martin Amerson Blamed George Zimmerman for Crime Before Killing Self," *Opposing Views*, August 4, 2013. Retrieved from www. opposingviews.com/i/society/guns/bank-robber-marvin-amerson-blamed-george-zimmerman-crime-killing-self#.

Chapter 5 Disposable Babies

1 "About Us," *The Prison Birth Project.* Retrieved from http://theprisonbirthproject. org/node/39.

2 D. Kasdan, "Abortion Access for Incarcerated Women: Are Correctional Health Practices in Conflict With Constitutional Standards?" *Perspectives on Sexual and Reproductive Health* 41, no. 1 (March 2009): 59–62; Carolyn B. Sufrin, Mitchell D. Creinin, and Judy C. Chang, "Incarcerated Mothers and Abortion Provision: A Survey of Correctional Health Providers," *Perspectives on Sexual and Reproductive Health* 41, no. 1 (March 2009): 6–11.

3 Deborah Allen and Brenda Baker, *Supporting Mothering Through Breastfeeding for Incarcerated Women* (Washington, D.C.: Association of Women's Health, Obstetric and Neonatal Nurses, 2013).

4 Women's Prison Association, *Mothers, Infants and Imprisonment: A National Look at Prison Nurseries and Community-based Alternatives* (New York: Women's Prison Association, 2009). Retrieved from http://66.29.139.159/pdf/Mothers%20 Infants%20and%20Imprisonment%202009.pdf.

5 Women's Prison Association, *Quick Facts: Women and Criminal Justice* (New York: Women's Prison Association, 2009). Retrieved from www.wpaonline.org/pdf/ Quick%20Facts%20Women%20and%20CJ_Sept09.pdf.

6 Ibid.

7 Rebecca Project for Human Rights and the National Women's Law Center, *Mothers Behind Bars: A State-by-State Report Card and Analysis of Federal Policies on Conditions of Confinement for Pregnant and Parenting Women and the Effect on Their Children* (Washington, D.C.: National Women's Law Center, 2010).

8 Richie, *Arrested Justice*, 57.

9 Victoria Law, "New Law Gives Parents Behind Bars in Washington State a Way to Hold Onto Their Children," *Truthout*, May 11, 2013. Retrieved from http://truth-out.org/news/item/16312-new-law-gives-parents-behind-bars-in-washington-state-a-way-to-hold-onto-their-children.

10 Dorothy E. Roberts. "Prison, Foster Care, and the Systemic Punishment of Black Mothers," *UCLA Law Review* 59 (2012): 1474.

11 Barbara Bloom, Barbara Owen, and Stephanie Covington, *Gender Responsive Strategies: Research, Practice, and Guiding Principles for Women Offenders* (Washington, D.C.: National Insitute of Correction, 2003).

12 Ajay Khashu, Timothy Ross, and Mark Wamsley, *Hard Data on Hard Times: An Empirical Analysis of Maternal Incarceration, Foster Care, and Visitation* (New York: Vera Institute of Justice, 2004).

13 Julie Poehlmann, "New Study Shows Children of Incarcerated Mothers

Experience Multiple Challenges," *Family Matters: A Family Impact Seminar Newsletter for Wisconsin Lawmakers* 3, no. 2 (October 2003). Retrieved from www.familyimpactseminars.org/fia_nlarticle_v3i2.pdf.

14 Drucker, *Plague of Prisons*, 131.

15 John Howard Association, *Monitoring Visits to Decatur Correctional Center 2013* (Chicago: John Howard Association, 2013). Retrieved from www.thejha.org/sites/default/files/Decatur_Correctional_Center_Report%202013.pdf.

16 Rebecca Project and National Women's Law Center, *Mothers Behind Bars*.

17 Women's Prison Association, Institute on Women and Criminal Justice, *Mothers, Infants and Imprisonment: A National Look at Prison Nurseries and Community-Based Alternatives* (New York: Chandra Kring Villanueva, 2009).

18 Creasie Finney Hairston, Robin E. Bates, and Shonda Lawrence-Willis, *Serving Incarcerated Mothers and Their Babies in Community-Based Residences* (Chicago: Jane Addams Center for Social Policy and Research, 2003).

19 Setsu Shigematsu, Gwen D'Arcangelis, Melissa Burch, "Prison Abolition in Practice: The LEAD Project, the Politics of Healing, and 'A New Way of Life.'" in *Abolition NOW! Ten Years of Strategy and Struggle Against the Prison Industrial Complex*, edited by CR10 Publications Collective (Oakland, Calif.: AK Press, 2008).

20 "The Lead Project," *A New Way of Life*, n.d., www.anewwayoflife.org/leadership-2/the-lead-project/.

21 "Milestones," *A New Way of Life*, n.d., http://anewwayoflife.org/milestones/.

22 Glenn E. Martin, "Marching Upstream: Moving Beyond Reentry Mania," in Mauer and Epstein, eds., *To Build a Better Criminal Justice System*, 48–49.

23 Angela Y. Davis, *The Angela Y. Davis Reader*, edited by Joy James (New York: Wiley, 1998), 218–19.

Chapter 6 The Case for a Pen Pal

1 Shelton, *Crossing the Yard*, 5.

2 Ibid., 6.

3 Ibid., 15.

4 Ibid., 9

5 Ibid., 64.

6 E. M. Forster, *The BBC Talks of E. M. Forster, 1929–1960: A Selected Edition*, ed. Mary Lago, Linda K. Hughes, and Elizabeth MacLeod Walls (Columbia: University of Missouri Press, 2008), 127.

7 Write to Win Collective: a prisoner correspondence project, n.d. Retrieved from: http://writetowin.wordpress.com.

Chapter 7 Working from the Inside Out: Decarcerate!

1 Amnesty International, "USA: Conditions Must Be Improved at Tamms Correctional Center in Illinois," March 25, 2009. Retrieved from www.amnesty.org/en/library/asset/AMR51/042/2009/en/22860b6c-a20b-4cc1-8485-2cbec988a725/amr510422009en.html.

2 *Solitary Watch*, "Fact Sheet: The High Cost of Solitary Confinement." Retrieved from: http://solitarywatch.com/wp-content/uploads/2011/06/fact-sheet-the-high-cost-of-solitary-confinement.pdf.

3 Project NIA, "Close Down Youth Prisons," 2012. Retrieved from http://closeyouthprisons.wordpress.com/2012/04/04/starve-the-p-i-c-2/.

4 Dan Berger, "Social Movements and Mass Incarceration: What Is to Be Done?," *Souls: A Critical Journal of Black Politics, Culture, and Society* 15, nos. 1–2 (Summer 2013): 3–18.

5 Matthew Heller, "Hunger Strike Sparks California Prison Reform Efforts," *MintPress News.* February 20, 2014.

6 John Howard Association, "Monitoring Visit to Lincoln Correctional Center," 2, July 2012, http://thejha.org/sites/default/files/Lincoln_Report.pdf.

7 James Austin, Wendy Ware, and Roger Ocker, *Orleans Parish Prison Ten-Year Inmate Population Projection.* Report prepared for National Criminal Justice Reference Service, Department of Justice (Denver: JFA-Associates, 2011). Retrieved from www.ncjrs.gov/pdffiles1/nij/grants/233722.pdf.

8 Orleans Parish Prison Project, "Mayor Plays Political Games at Our Peril," April 18, 2013. Retrieved from http://opprc.wordpress.com/2013/04/18/mayor-plays-political-games-at-our-peril/.

9 T. Minton, *Data Collection: Annual Survey of Jails* (Washington, D.C.: Bureau of Justice Statistics, 2012).

10 Jamie Fellner, *The Price of Freedom: Bail and Pretrial Detention of Low Income Nonfelony Defendants in New York City* (New York: Human Rights Watch, 2010), 2.

11 Cynthia E. Jones, "'Give Us Free': Addressing Racial Disparities in Bail Determinations," *New York University Journal of Legislation and Public Policy* 16 (2013): 919–61.

12 Fellner, *The Price of Freedom*, 31.

13 "Virginia's Justice System: Expensive, Ineffective and Unfair," Justice Policy Institute, November 2013, 11. Retrieved from www.justicepolicy.org/uploads/justicepolicy/documents/va_justice_system_expensive_ineffective_and_unfair_final.pdf.

14 Mariame Kaba, "Prison Reform's In Vogue & Other Strange Things..." *Prison Culture: How the PIC Structures Our World*, March 2014. Retrieved from: http://www.usprisonculture.com/blog/2014/03/18/prison-reforms-in-vogue-other-strange-things/.

15 California Department of Corrections and Rehabilitation, "Realignment," December 2013. Retrieved from www.cdcr.ca.gov/realignment/.

16 CURB Prison Spending, "Realignment Report Card," November 2013. Retrieved from http://curbprisonspending.org/?p=3403.

17 "Priority Issues: Law Enforcement," Right on Crime, 2010. Retrieved from www.rightoncrime.com/priority-issues/law-enforcement/.

Chapter 8 Telling Stories

1 Davis, *Angela Y. Davis Reader*, 105.

2 Illinois Disproportionate Justice Impact Study Commission, *Key Findings and Recommendations*, 2011. Retrieved from www.senatedem.ilga.gov/phocadownload/PDF/Attachments/2011/djisfactsheet.pdf.

3 Rosie Teague and Paul Mazerolle, *Childhood Physical Abuse and Adult Offending: Are They Linked, and Is There Scope for Early Intervention?* (Brisbane, Queensland: Crime and Misconduct Coalition, 2007).

4 Madeline Wordes and Mitchell Nunez, *Our Vulnerable Teenagers: Their Victimization, Its Consequences, and Directions for Prevention and Intervention* (Oakland, Calif.: National Center for Victims of Crime, 2010). Retrieved from www.victimsofcrime.org/docs/Documents/teen_victim_report.pdf?sfvrsn=0.

5 Philly Stand Up, "The Accountability Roadmap," *The Abolitionist* 16 (n.d.): 7–8.

6 Sara Kershnar et al., *Toward Transformative Justice: A Liberatory Approach to Child Sexual Abuse and Other Forms of Community Violence* (San Francisco: Generation FIVE, 2007). Retrieved from www.generationfive.org/wp-content/uploads/2013/07/G5_Toward_Transformative_Justice-Document.pdf.

7 Angela J. Davis, *Arbitrary Justice: The Power of the American Prosecutor* (New York: Oxford University Press, 2008), 70.

8 "Kalispell, Montana (MT) Poverty Rate Data: Information About Poor and Low-Income Residents," City-data.com, n.d. Retrieved from www.city-data.com/poverty/poverty-Kalispell-Montana.html; "Kalispell, MT Politics and Election Data," *Home Facts*, 2013. Retrieved from www.homefacts.com/politics/Montana/Flathead-County/Kalispell.html.

9 Timothy B. Conley, Kimberley Spurzen, Eamon Marsh, and Jessica Hazlett, *Juvenile Offenders in Montana: Risk Level, Probation Status and Recidivism* (Missoula: University of Montana, 2009), 12.

10 "About Us," *Center for Restorative Youth Justice*, n.d., www.restorativeyouthjustice.org/about.

11 Joanna Shapland et al., "Situating Restorative Justice Within Criminal Justice," *Theoretical Criminology* 10, no. 4 (2006): 505–32.

12 "FAQ," *Philly Stands Up!*, 2010. Retrieved from www.phillystandsup.com/faq.html.

13 "Community Responds to Domestic Violence," *Creative Interventions: Storytelling & Organizing Project*, n.d. Retrieved from www.stopviolenceeveryday.org/wp-content/uploads/community%20responds%20to%20domestic%20violence.pdf.

14 Los Angeles Incite! / LA COIL / Youth Justice Coalition / Dignity and Power Now/People's Education Movement / CURB, "Transformative Justice Strategies for Addressing Police/Vigilante / Hate/White Supremacist Violence: Working Document," January 2014. Retrieved from http://andrea366.wordpress.com/2014/02/08/transformative-justice-strategies-for-addressing-policevigilantehatewhite-supremacist-violence/.

Chapter 9 The Peace Room

1 Andrea Smith, "Captured by the State: The Antiviolence Movement and the Nonprofit Industrial Complex," Keynote at the 9th Annual Critical Race and Anti-Colonial Studies Conference, Concordia University, Montreal, Quebec, June 2009.

2 Robin M. Steans, "School Violence Report Needs Context," *Catalyst Chicago*, December 1, 2007, www.catalyst-chicago.org/news/2007/11/29/school-violence-report-needs-context.

3 Mariame Kaba and Eva Nagao, *Policing Chicago Public Schools: Gateway to the School-to-Prison Pipeline* (Chicago: Project NIA, 2012).

4 "Restorative Justice," *Umoja Corporation*, n.d., http://umojacorporation.org/our-approach/restorative-justice/.

5 *Civil Rights Data Collection* (Washington, D.C.: Office for Civil Rights, US Department of Education, 2012).

6 Micky Duxbury, "Circles of Change: Bringing a More Compassionate Justice System to Troubled Youth in Oakland," *The Monthly* (March 2011). Retrieved from http://berkeleymonthly.net/upfront1103.html.

7 Project NIA, "Over 50,000 CPS Students Suspended in 2010–11," *Suspension Stories*,

November 30, 2011. Retrieved from www.suspensionstories.com/2011/11/30/cps-administered-over-40000-out-of-school-suspension-in-2010-11/.

8 International Institute for Restorative Practices, *Improving School Climate: Findings from "Schools Implementing Restorative Practices,"* 2009. Retrieved from www.iirp.edu/pdf/IIRP-Improving-School-Climate.pdf.

9 Umoja Corporation, "Fact Sheet: Restorative Justice," n.d.; www.umojacorporation.org/files/5413/5402/9632/Fact_Sheet_RestorativeJustice_PBIS.pdf.

10 Moira Kenney, *Mapping Gay L.A.: The Intersection of Place and Politics* (Philadelphia: Temple University Press, 2001), 24.

11 Christina B. Hanhardt, *Safe Space: Gay Neighborhood History and the Politics of Violence* (Durham, N.C.: Duke University Press, 2013).

12 Angela Caputo, "Cell Blocks," *Chicago Reporter*, March 1, 2013.

13 Molly Wahlberg, "Historian Sees Beauty Shops as Birthplace of Activism," University of Texas Department of History. Retrieved from www.utexas.edu/cola/depts/history/features/past-features/gill-beauty-shop-politics10.php.

14 Dorothy Tucker, "Chicago Neighborhood Training Hairstylists to Act as Peacekeepers," *CBS 2 Chicago*, June 10, 2013.

15 "Safe Neighborhood Campaign," *The Audre Lorde Project*, http://alp.org/safe-neighborhood-campaign.

16 Di Grennell, "Ha Korero Iti: A Small Story," *Creative Interventions: Storytelling & Organizing Project*. Retrieved from www.stopviolenceeveryday.org/he-korero-iti-%E2%80%93-a-small-story/.

Chapter 10 A Wakeup

1 Davis, "Masked Racism."

2 Lisa Marie Alatorre and Chanelle Gallant, "CKUT Interview with the Co-Editors of Everyday Abolition," *Everyday Abolition/Abolition Every Day*, June 2013. Retrieved from http://everydayabolition.com/2013/09/16/ckut-interview-with-the-co-editors-of-everyday-abolition-abolition-everyday/.

3 Micha Cárdenas, "Finding the Movements That Keep Us Safe," *Everyday Abolition/Abolition Every Day*, August 30, 2013. Retrieved from http://everydayabolition.com/2013/08/30/finding-the-movements-that-keep-us-safe/.

4 Benedict Carey, "Holding Loved One's Hand Can Calm Jittery Neurons," *New York Times*, January 31, 2006.

5 Dan Berger, "Social Movements and Mass Incarceration," *Souls: A Critical Journal of Black Politics, Culture, and Society* 15, nos. 1–2 (July 2013): 3–18.

6 Quinn Ford, "West Garfield Park Parents, Religious Leaders Protest School Closings," *DNAInfo Chicago*, March 30, 2013.

7 Gaëlle Faure, "Why Doctors Are Giving Heroin to Drug Addicts," *Time*, September 28, 2009.

8 Amy Goodman, "Angela Davis on the Prison Abolishment Movement," *Democracy Now*, October 19, 2010.

Epilogue Not an Ending

1 Jewell Oates, "Second Chances: Life at the Women's Treatment Center," *Women's Treatment Center Newsletter*, Fall 2011, www.womenstreatmentcenter.org/_files/content/pdfs/twtcfall2011newsletter_201205211523485038.pdf.

Resources

Books

Abolition Now! Ten Years of Strategy and Struggle Against the Prison-Industrial Complex, by the CR-10 Publishing Collective (Oakland: AK Press, 2008)
This compilation honors the work of Critical Resistance, a collective that works toward PIC abolition. The book's themes are "Dismantle," "Change," and "Build," and its essays put forth courageous ideas and highlight movements for transformation.

Are Prisons Obsolete? by Angela Y. Davis (New York: Seven Stories, 2003)
In this pithy, powerful book, Angela Davis makes a clear-cut case that prisons should be abolished. She looks at how past movements made slavery, the convict-lease program, and overt racial segregation "obsolete" practices and suggests the time has come for prisons to go that route as well.

Arrested Justice: Black Women, Violence, and America's Prison Nation, by Beth Richie (New York: New York University Press, 2012)
This book documents the suffering of black women at the hands of male violence—at both the intimate and state levels—and how the white feminist antiviolence movement has failed them. Richie demonstrates how state responses to gender violence often criminalize and punish survivors themselves.

Beyond Walls and Cages: Prisons, Borders and Global Crisis,
edited by Jenna M. Loyd, Matt Mitchelson, and Andrew Burridge
(Athens: University of Georgia Press, 2012)
Linking the prison-industrial complex and the violent policies and practices that govern migration, this collection advocates an approach to activism that connects the prison abolition and immigrant justice movements.

Captive Genders: Trans Embodiment and the Prison Industrial Complex,
edited Eric A. Stanley and Nat Smith (Oakland: AK Press, 2011)
This collection focuses on how the practices of the prison-industrial complex impact trans, gender-nonconforming, and queer people. It calls for a recognition that the struggles for prison abolition and trans and queer liberation are inextricably linked.

Golden Gulag: Prisons, Surplus, Crisis, and Opposition in Globalizing California, by Ruth Gilmore (Berkeley: University of California Press, 2007)
In this detailed account of the rise of mass incarceration in California, Gilmore looks at its roots in financial shifts, racism, and the repression of social movements.

High Price: A Neuroscientist's Journey of Self-Discovery That Challenges Everything You Know about Drugs and Society, by Carl Hart
(New York: Harper, 2013)
This book combines neuroscience and memoir to take down antidrug propaganda. It shows how pointing to drug abuse as the root of societal ills serves as a decoy that simply fuels incarceration and distracts from real social problems.

Imprisoning Communities: How Mass Incarceration Makes Disadvantaged Neighborhoods Worse, by Todd Clear (New York: Oxford University Press, 2007)
This intensively researched text spells out the implications of large-scale imprisonment for poor neighborhoods, primarily neighborhoods of color.

A Kind and Just Parent: The Children of the Juvenile Court,
by Bill Ayers (Boston: Beacon Press, 1998)
Ayers chronicles his experiences teaching and observing in Chicago's juvenile detention center, telling the stories of the individual kids he came to know and revealing the necessity of systemic change.

Lockdown America: Police and Prisons in the Age of Crisis, 2nd edn.,
by Christian Parenti (London: Verso, 2008)
Mass incarceration's economic underpinnings are the emphasis of
this sweeping work. Parenti argues that the rise of the "police state" is
closely tied to the "managing" of surplus populations created by hyper-
capitalism.

The New Jim Crow: Mass Incarceration in the Age of Color-Blindness,
by Michelle Alexander (New York: New Press, 2010)
This groundbreaking book demonstrates how mass incarceration—like
slavery and the Jim Crow laws—serves to maintain a racial "caste system."
Alexander focuses on the impact of the drug war on black men, and the
far-reaching impacts of that targeting.

Resistance Behind Bars: The Struggles of Incarcerated Women,
by Victoria Law (Oakland: PM Press, 2009)
Focusing on activism initiated by women in prison, this book provides
a much-needed look at individual and collective struggles that are rarely
made visible beyond the walls of prison.

Action Resources

All of Us or None
www.allofusornone.org
1540 Market Street, Suite 490
San Francisco, CA 94102
This organization advocates for the rights of incarcerated and formerly
incarcerated people and their families, organizing around such issues as
record expungement, voting rights, and opposing employment discrimination and jail expansion.

Audre Lorde Project
www.alp.org
147 West 24th Street, 3rd Floor
New York, NY 10011
The Audre Lorde Project is a lesbian, gay, bisexual, trans and gender-
nonconforming people of color community organizing center. The Project
includes Safe OUTside the System, an antiviolence program that utilizes
community justice strategies.

Black and Pink
www.blackandpink.org
614 Columbia Road
Dorchester, MA 02125
Black & Pink works to advocate for LGBTQ prisoners and to act against
the system as a whole, through the lens of LGBTQ justice. It distributes
a free monthly newspaper to prisoners and also leads a pen-pal project.

California Families to Abolish Solitary Confinement
www.abolishsolitary.org,
c/o FACTS Education Fund
1137 E. Redondo Blvd.
Inglewood, CA 90302
Born during the 2011 Pelican Bay hunger strike, CFASC aims to end the
use of solitary confinement. In the short term, the group pushes to reduce
the practice and advocates for the demands of prisoners held in isolation.

Campaign to End the New Jim Crow
www.endnewjimcrow.org
The Riverside Church
490 Riverside Drive
New York, NY 10027
A joint project of the American Friends Service Committee and the Riverside Church Prison Ministry, this organization works to end mass incarceration through education, direct action, and coalition-building.

Creative Interventions
www.creative-interventions.org
4390 Telegraph Avenue, #A
Oakland, CA 94609
This site is filled with resources and strategies for preventing and responding to interpersonal violence, outside of policing and prison. It offers an
in-depth, practical toolkit on violence prevention.

Critical Resistance
www.criticalresistance.org
1904 Franklin Street, Suite 504
Oakland, CA 94612
CR, a national grassroots movement, works to end the prison-industrial
complex and build stable, healthy communities. The group approaches the
goal of abolition through three frames: dismantle, change, and build.

CURB Prisons
www.curbprisonspending.org
P.O. Box 73688
Los Angeles, CA 90003
Californians United for a Responsible Budget (CURB) is a coalition of more than forty organizations aiming to decrease the number of people in prison and the number of prisons in the state of California.

Decarcerate IL
www.nationinside.org/campaign/decarcerate-illinois
This group, which grew out of the recent series of Illinois prison closures, works to reduce incarceration in the state and to urge investment in prison alternatives.

Decarcerate PA
www.decarceratepa.info
P.O. Box 40764
Philadelphia, PA 19107
This campaign works to end mass incarceration in Pennsylvania, pushing for the state to stop building prisons; reduce the prison population; and reinvest in community priorities like education, housing, and health care.

Everyday Abolition
www.everydayabolition.com
This international political art collaboration features a blog based on the ways people are "living abolition" in their everyday lives.

Ex-Prisoners and Prisoners Organizing for Community Advancement
www.exprisoners.org
This Massachusetts group organizes against policies that harm people with criminal records, pushes for sentencing reform, and runs the Jobs NOT Jails campaign aimed at redirecting money from incarceration to addressing unemployment.

INCITE! Women of Color Against Violence
www.inciteblog.wordpress.com
INCITE! is a national organization of radical feminists of color advancing a movement to end violence through direct action, critical dialogue, and grassroots organizing.

Nation Inside: www.nationinside.org
This online platform hosts campaigns that challenge mass incarceration. You can join a campaign in your area, read stories of people who've been impacted by the prison-industrial complex, and share your own story or perspective.

Prison Culture: www.usprisonculture.com
This blog tracks the workings of the prison-industrial complex, providing news, analysis, and action items in the anti-PIC struggle.

Prison Legal News and *Human Rights Defense Center*
www.prisonlegalnews.org and www.humanrightsdefensecenter.org
P.O. Box 1151
Lake Worth, FL 33460
Prison Legal News prints news and analysis of issues relating to prisoners, and it's widely read in prisons. It is sponsored by Human Rights Defense Center, a nonprofit that advocates for incarcerated people's rights.

Project NIA:
www.project-nia.org
This Chicago-based project combines organizing, education, research, and advocacy, working toward the goal of ending youth incarceration and building community-based models of addressing youth crime.

Release Aging People in Prison:
www.rappcampaign.com
The Correctional Association of New York
2090 Adam Clayton Powell Blvd., 2nd Floor
New York, NY 10027
RAPP advocates for the establishment of a fair parole process in New York, and for other decarceration-focused policy changes. The group aims to increase the number of incarcerated elders who are released from prison.

Sylvia Rivera Law Project
www.srlp.org
147 West 24th Street, 5th Floor
New York, NY 10011
SRLP provides access to legal services for low-income transgender, intersex, and gender nonconforming people, and engages in action directed at ending institutional violence and discrimination based on gender identity and expression.

Get a Pen Pal!

Black and Pink
www.blackandpink.org
614 Columbia Road
Dorchester, MA 02125

November Coalition
www.november.org; write to Nora, at nora[AT]November.org
282 West Astor Avenue
Colville, WA 99114

Prisoner Correspondence Project
www.prisonercorrespondenceproject.com/
QPIRG Concordia c/o Concordia University
1455 de Maisonneuve O, Montreal, QC H3G 1M8
Canada

Women's Prison Book Project
www.wpbp.org/
c/o Boneshaker Books
2002 23rd Avenue S.
Minneapolis, MN 55404

Write a Prisoner
www.writeaprisoner.com/inmate-profiles
P.O. Box 10
Edgewater, FL 32132

Write to Win Collective
http://writetowin.wordpress.com/
2040 N. Milwaukee Avenue
Chicago, IL 60647

Acknowledgments

I couldn't have written a word of this book without the wisdom and generosity of the following people. Their insights and stories, gleaned through interviews, correspondence, guidance, long conversations, and friendships, are what brought this book into existence. Thank you to my sister, my parents, Hakim Ali, April Anderson, Bill Ayers, Sue Barrow, Dan Berger, Kate Berry, Reginald Akkeem Berry, Katie Boyd, Lillie Branch-Kennedy, Nora Callahan, Beth Derenne, Jake Donaghy, Diane Dwyer, Bill and Kimberly Emerson, Barbara Fair, Eugene Fischer, Jimmy Flores, Chanelle Gallant, Marcos Gray, Sarah Grey, Lacino Hamilton, Carl Hart, Jazz Hayden, Joe Jackson, Dahr Jamail, Deborah Jiang-Stein, Tiffany Johnson, Mariame Kaba, Fr. David Kelly, Kathy Kelly, Alice Kim, Sable Sade Kolstee, Victoria Law, Rev. Jason Lydon, Abraham Macías Jr., Glenn E. Martin, Donna McNeil, Layne Mullett, Peter Newman, Nick Nyman, Isaac Ontiveros, Jenna Peters-Golden, Laurie Jo Reynolds, Beth Richie, Kenny

Riley, Carlos Rodriguez, Mauricio Rueben, Miguel Segarra, Andrea Smith, Gabrielle Stout, Lawson Strickland, Audrey Stuart, Nick Szuberla, Susan Garcia Treischmann, Alok Vaid-Menon, Johnnie Walton, Claudia Whitman, Tasha Wilkerson, Steven Michael Woods, Ilana Zafran, and Diana Zuñiga.

To the Berrett-Koehler staff: Thank you for welcoming me into your wonderful community, and for treating me and my book with so much kindness, care, and respect throughout this process. To the folks at the Lannan Foundation: I came to my residency with barely a chapter and came out with a draft of a book—I'm inexpressibly grateful. To the *Truthout* staff: Your brilliance and dedication inspires me every day, and I'm honored and humbled by your support for this project! And thank you to Ryan, for responding to my daily announcements of "I can't write a book!" with daily groans—plus compassion, encouragement, and love. Finally, my gratitude goes out to all the people who are working, day by day, to build movements for liberation and justice.

Index

About the Author

Maya Schenwar is Editor-in-Chief of *Truthout*, an independent social justice news website. She has written about the prison-industrial complex for *Truthout*, the *New York Times*, the *Guardian*, the *New Jersey Star-Ledger*, *Ms.* magazine, and others. She is the recipient of a Society of Professional Journalists Sigma Chi Award and a Lannan Residency Fellowship, both for her writing on  prisons. Previous to her work at *Truthout*, Maya was Contributing Editor at *Punk Planet* magazine and served as media coordinator for Voices for Creative Nonviolence.

Berrett–Koehler
Publishers

Berrett-Koehler is an independent publisher dedicated to an ambitious mission: *Creating a World That Works for All.*

We believe that to truly create a better world, action is needed at all levels—individual, organizational, and societal. At the individual level, our publications help people align their lives with their values and with their aspirations for a better world. At the organizational level, our publications promote progressive leadership and management practices, socially responsible approaches to business, and humane and effective organizations. At the societal level, our publications advance social and economic justice, shared prosperity, sustainability, and new solutions to national and global issues.

A major theme of our publications is "Opening Up New Space." Berrett-Koehler titles challenge conventional thinking, introduce new ideas, and foster positive change. Their common quest is changing the underlying beliefs, mindsets, institutions, and structures that keep generating the same cycles of problems, no matter who our leaders are or what improvement programs we adopt.

We strive to practice what we preach—to operate our publishing company in line with the ideas in our books. At the core of our approach is stewardship, which we define as a deep sense of responsibility to administer the company for the benefit of all of our "stakeholder" groups: authors, customers, employees, investors, service providers, and the communities and environment around us.

We are grateful to the thousands of readers, authors, and other friends of the company who consider themselves to be part of the "BK Community." We hope that you, too, will join us in our mission.

A BK Currents Book

This book is part of our BK Currents series. BK Currents books advance social and economic justice by exploring the critical intersections between business and society. Offering a unique combination of thoughtful analysis and progressive alternatives, BK Currents books promote positive change at the national and global levels. To find out more, visit **www.bkconnection.com**.

Berrett–Koehler
Publishers

A community dedicated to creating
a world that works for all

Dear Reader,

Thank you for picking up this book and joining our worldwide community of Berrett-Koehler readers. We share ideas that bring positive change into people's lives, organizations, and society.

To welcome you, we'd like to offer you a free e-book. You can pick from among twelve of our bestselling books by entering the promotional code **BKP92E** here: http://www.bkconnection.com/welcome.

When you claim your free e-book, we'll also send you a copy of our e-newsletter, the *BK Communiqué*. Although you're free to unsubscribe, there are many benefits to sticking around. In every issue of our newsletter you'll find

- A free e-book
- Tips from famous authors
- Discounts on spotlight titles
- Hilarious insider publishing news
- A chance to win a prize for answering a riddle

Best of all, our readers tell us, "Your newsletter is the only one I actually read." So claim your gift today, and please stay in touch!

Sincerely,

Charlotte Ashlock
Steward of the BK Website

Questions? Comments? Contact me at bkcommunity@bkpub.com.